TRUE STORIES
of Elmira, New York

Volume 1

By James Hare & Diane Janowski

This book is a selection of their freelance articles
in the Elmira *Star-Gazette*

True Stories of Elmira, New York, Volume 1

ISBN: 978-0-9994192-0-5

Printed in the United States of America

First Edition

Cover image: Postcard view of Elmira, East Water Street from the Hulette Building. Publisher unknown.

Dedicated to our better halves -
as they have to live with historians.....

Alicia G. Hare
Denny Smith

Table of Contents

All Quiet on the Elmiran Front

by Diane L. Janowski

In 1942 homefront Elmirans were worried that World War II could end up on our doorsteps. We were afraid of enemy planes coming with a surprise attack. Elmira's Civil Defense Council believed that citizens should be ready for anything, so it organized a practice blackout drill for Sunday, January 4 from 9:35 to 9:45 PM. Potential enemy attackers would not see Elmira from the air if all lights were off, and would have tested Elmira's readiness for a possible enemy attack. Elmira Heights and Horseheads would also take part.

The Chairman of Defense Council Edgar Austin said, "Let's take this practice seriously, because some day it might mean your life or mine. Without a test, we won't know how we stand."

Two days before the test, the Defense Council provided the rules for an organized blackout:

1. *Keep cool - avoid disorder - cooperate with the air warden.*
2. *Be home if possible. If you are on the street - walk - not run - home.*
3. *The Power Company will pull NO master switches, except those operating the streetlights. Do NOT shut off the current in your home.*
4. *Put out all unnecessary lights, screen all windows where necessary lights are kept burning.*
5. *If you will not be at home, make certain all lights off before leaving.*
6. *Lock all doors and windows.*
7. *Make no unnecessary telephone calls.*
8. *Should an emergency arise, call the police directly.*
9. *Disregard all telephone calls announcing an air raid or blackout. Disregard all but official warnings.*
10. *If you are driving when warning sounds, pull to the curb at once and extinguish auto lights.*

All this talk about the enemy and the blackout drill riled up Elmirans into an anti-Japanese/German frenzy. Elmirans hastily organized "blackout parties" and hurried invitations went out on Saturday. Newspaper advertisements announced sales for curtains and Venetian blinds.

On Sunday, an hour or more before the blackout, hundreds of Elmirans left their homes to stake out positions on East Hill, Mount Zoar, West Hill, and other sites overlooking the city to enjoy the beauty of the test. East Hill Road and Jerusalem Hill Road were jammed with automobiles. The Elmira Camera Club photographed the stages of the blackout from various high stations around the area. Thousands of pedestrians filled downtown Elmira and wandered around satisfying their curiosity about what would happen.

Factory whistles around the area sounded the warning, and the blackout happened as scheduled at 9:35 PM. Lights dimmed in the city and surrounding area. Southside residents did not hear the warning whistles - apparently because of the distance of the factories, but took the cue when the streetlights went out. The blackout lasted exactly ten minutes.

On the next day, the newspapers reported that the results of the blackout drill were "practically perfect" except for the use of the factory whistles to alert Elmirans. The whistles were not loud enough for everyone to hear. Except for a few cases, citizens extinguished their lights properly.

Later that year, Elmira experienced a mock air raid drill. On May 17, the War Council scheduled an air raid drill with "enemy" planes over the skies of Elmira. Other planned "disasters" were to happen on the ground. Elmira's War Council said that "the exact hour and duration are secret, but it will not begin until the church-going public has returned home." The Council issued the following rules:

1. *If driving - draw up to the curb and remain there until the "all clear."*
2. *If walking - seek shelter immediately.*
3. *Obey orders of official volunteers wearing distinctive armbands.*

With the disappointing warning whistles of the blackout drill, a revised plan implementing more factory whistles, along with a new whistles installed on Cowles Hall at Elmira College and on City Hall.

At 11:15 AM, after many Elmirans had returned from church, the "air raid" began, and except for an unexplained delay in the "enemy planes,"

Water St., East of Main Before and During Blackout

W. WATER ST. was dark during Sunday night's blackout except for one store at right in which lights blazed on. Main St. was completely blacked out.

From the Elmira *Star-Gazette* January 5, 1942 page 9.

the wardens conducted the drill without a major fault. The whistle system announced the sighted planes.

Behind City Hall, in the parking lot, the wardens organized a mock riot. Captain John Fiester supplied the group with wooden guns. The "riot squad," consisting of Elmira Reformatory guards, used real tear gas to subdue the "rioters" feigning hand-to-hand combat. Some real injuries happened in the fracas, and the "riot" ended with the capture of Captain Fiester.

A mock fire disaster was staged at the City Rescue Mission on William Street. Elmira's fire fighters were tested for their speed of getting to and extinguishing a fire. When the "fire call" came into the Fire Department, the fire fighters left the station and drove to the site. There, they unrolled their hoses, turned on the water, and extinguish the "fire" on the front lawn of the Mission. It took four minutes.

The Elmira Rescue Squad responded to a call of a victim "trapped" on Clinton Island in the Chemung River. Another rescue came in for 411 Railroad Avenue, where two men were "trapped" under timbers on the third floor. Later, the Squad responded to the shale quarry on East Hill for some "suspicious" activities, which turned out to be two real young couples having a romantic picnic.

There was a simulated water main break, and a "large bomb crater" at the north end of Lake Street Bridge. About 1,200 volunteers helped in the day's activities.

Lieutenant Colonel John Johnson of the State War Council said, "This is an example of what the public may expect at any time, particularly because Elmira is such a vital industrial area." Johnson also commented that our audible whistle system was a "hopeless failure with three-quarters of the community unable to know a raid was on if they were not expecting one." He did express astonishment over the almost complete absence of motor traffic and pedestrians and gave the highest praise for the work of the auxiliary police and the air raid wardens.

Source:
Elmira *Star-Gazette/Sunday Telegram*, January 1-5, 1942, and May 15-18, 1942.

Adopting the City Manager Plan

By James Hare

You Want Better Government; Will You Help City Get It?

The city manager plan of city government is the most efficient, economical, modern way of governing cities. Do you want it adopted in Elmira? Are you willing to do your share to help get it? Then please sign the coupon below and mail or bring it to The Star-Gazette office.

A generally aroused, earnest citizenry can have what it wills, if it is willing to work for it. Signing this coupon is the first step in making Elmira government better.

I am FOR the city manager plan of government in Elmira.

Name ....
                      (Write clearly or print)

Street and No. ....

Coupon in Elmira *Star-Gazette* on February 11, 1932 page 3.

"If we have city manager government will it get rid of the present alderman?" A woman inquired over the telephone.

"Yes," was the reply.

"Then I'm for it. I'll send in my coupon." She said.

So reported the Elmira *Star-Gazette* on February 11, 1932, promoting its coupon campaign in favor of a city manager plan of government. Frank E. Tripp, publisher of the paper, and one of the sponsors of the movement, declared in a published statement March 7th, "the main motives in the minds of those who favor City Management are to stop waste of city funds, reduce city debt, give the city a simplified city government, eliminate politics in city affairs and hereby give the citizen more for his money and reduce taxes."

In the middle of the Great Depression, Elmira faced serious fiscal problems. As of January 1, 1932, Auditor Francis N. Mullen reported to the

Common Council a deficit of $399,447.27. He stated that the years 1930-31 were "poorly administered, both in budget planning and in the adminis-trative control..." A month later, the newly elected mayor, Glen Sweet, noted that many city employees were in "destitute circumstances" as they had not been paid since mid November. By March, four city officials would resign because of enforcement of a state law that they could not hold office and do direct or indirect business with the city. The city budget had doubled since 1921, growing from $549,275 to $922,622.50 in 1931. The proposed 1932 budget of $1,124,083.04 called for a 48% tax increase from $17.94 to $26.49. In addition, Governor Roosevelt refused to sanction a deficiency bond issue to cover the deficit. The local Real Estate Board publicly op-posed any tax rate over $20.03.

Elmira was operating under a government with a mayor elected at large, with twelve alderman representing wards based on a 1906 charter, one of the oldest in the state. In 1916, the city had rejected changing to a commission form of government. Mayor Sweet, soon after taking office, appointed a Charter Revision Committee. In March, Attorney Hubert C. Mandeville, a member of the committee, would report that, "the key of our plan is to make the mayor responsible directly to the people (mayor - 4-year term, alderman - 2-year term) and give him the power so he cannot escape responsibility."

The battle had been joined prior to the Mandeville report. The *Star-Gazette* had over 3000 responses to its pro Plan C coupon campaign. In early March a mass meeting of Elmirans had been held to endorse the movement. From that meeting a 25 member City Manager Plan Commit-tee was formed, led by Homer E. Brotzman and A. D. Merrill. Their task was to organize a petition drive calling for a referendum to adopt Plan C. Within days of that meeting 5,235 signatures had been gathered calling for a referendum.

On March 8, 1932, the Common Council set May 5th for a spe-cial election. There was debate over the cost of such an election. Alder-man Wood M. Rickolt said the Star Gazette should be blamed. "They been razzing the Council members for spending too much money... they been hollering about how much we spent. Now they ask us to spend more on an election." The city would borrow $7,000 to cover expenses.

In addition to cost, the issues involved were many. Would an "outside expert" be a better manager than a person elected from the community? Should the council be elected "at large" or by districts? How many council members should there be? Herbert L. Ray, former assistant corporate counsel of Binghamton, spoke to a crowd of "less than 100 people" claimed, "city manager government is a form of despotism. All the power is invested in one man. The result is satisfactory if he is honest—quite the opposite if he is not."

The campaign was contentious. The *Star-Gazette* warned voters to "beware of 11th hour tactics by politicians opposed to the City Manager Plan...one man reported he had been asked by a city official to go out to work against Plan C tomorrow and that he would be paid for it... the workers for the City Manager Plan are all voluntary."

On May 5, 1932 Elmirans voted 5,074 to 4,280 for the Plan C form of government. Seven of twelve wards were supportive, sweeping the four wards on the Southside. Florence J. Sullivan (Sully to his admirers), a member of the mayor's Charter Revision Committee, manager of the incinerating plant, and an opponent of Plan C became the first City Manager on January 1, 1934. According to County Historian Tom Bryne, "the Police, Fire and Welfare commissions and the Board of Public Works were abolished and their powers conferred on the city manager." Upon leaving office in 1937 Sullivan became an executive of the NYS. Electric and Gas Corporation. Over time there have been revisions in the plan. Today the City of Elmira has six councilmembers elected by district with the mayor elected at large. The Council and Mayor serve four year terms and appoint the City Manager, who becomes the Chief Executive Officer. For those who want government to be run like a business, the concept is that the Council and Mayor are the board of directors and the manager is the executive carrying out policy.

Based on figures kept by the International City/County Management Association, 62% of the cities in the U.S. with a population between 25,000 and 50,000 use the council manager form of government as of 2014.

More about the Chemung Canal

By Diane Janowski

We've all heard about the Chemung Canal – how it connected Elmira to Watkins Glen, Seneca Lake, the Erie Canal and all points from there. We know that it followed today's Clemens Center Parkway in downtown Elmira. But what was it really, how did it work, what did a canal boat look like?

The Chemung Canal was literally a hand-dug ditch about twenty miles in length. It was forty-two feet

The Chemung Canal around 1865.
Image courtesy of the Barnes Library.

wide at the surface, twenty-six feet wide at the base, and four feet in depth. The project began in 1830 and took three years to complete. With 443 feet in elevation differences – the canal had forty-nine locks, five locks between Elmira and Horseheads (the highest point), twenty-one locks from Horseheads to Millport, and twenty-three locks between Millport and Montour Falls.

To provide the water necessary for depth at the high point in Horse-heads, a feeder canal drew water from the Chemung River below Corning. The feeder canal crossed Big Flats with three locks and joined the Chemung Canal near Hanover Square.

After four years of debate in the state legislature, final approval for the canal came in 1829. Elmira businessmen and local farmers rejoiced.

Elmira held a huge celebration with lots of food and alcohol . Now their goods would be shipped to bigger markets and supplies ordered could be more easily delivered.

Work began smoothly in 1830 and a half-mile section in Horseheads was quickly finished. The soil was sandy and easy to dig. Workers used picks, shovels, and wheelbarrows to move the dirt. In Millport, the soil was so sandy that it easily collapsed. Landslides along the canal were commonplace. Three workers were killed when a high embankment collapsed. Subcontractors bid on sections, making each section different from each other. Accepted bids were much lower than actual costs. Corners were cut. It was hard to keep labor as three other canals were being built regionally. Laborers moved around to get the best wage.

Workers were mostly Irish who did not like being here. They missed Ireland and were treated poorly by the overseers and the locals. They worked from morning to night, seven days a week. They lived in shanties along the canal. Whiskey was provided during work as an incentive to lessen the burden of the tough conditions. Murders and assaults were common on the canal. Stores popped up all along the canal for the convenience of the workers. Cash only.

By early summer 1832, digging the canal was complete, but a problem arose. Clay had been used to line the banks so the canal could hold water. The first test proved that several sections of the canal leaked. The water was drained and the sections repaired.

Another problem arose. In order to save money the locks were made of wood instead of the recommended stone. The locks leaked and bowed. They had to be repaired before they could be used. Crews worked all through the winter and the canal finally opened in May 1833.

Trouble again set in on May 5, 1833 when a torrential two day rain storm caused enough damage to close the canal. Some banks had to be rebuilt. It took until November to completely fix the problems and reopen the canal. But, the canal had to close in December because of winter.

Although Elmira had several boat builders that produced canal boats, Millport supported six boatyards. Because the Chemung Canal was a small canal, boats were specially made for navigation. According to Gary

Emerson's Link in the Great Chain, there were two types of vessel: "lakers" with curved bows and "scows" with straight bows. Both were made of pine planks. Chemung Canal boats were about sixty-feet long and fifteen-feet wide, the width to accommodate the passing of boats going either direction. Horses or mules slept in the bow area. Workers and passengers cooked and slept in the stern area. These boats were much smaller than boats used on the Erie Canal.

The canal made money for a short while, but because of the high costs of repairs and the arrival of the railroad through our region, it was not very profitable. To get from Elmira to Watkins Glen on the canal was difficult. A towpath along side the canal allowed horses or mules to pull the canal boats. It was a nearly twenty-mile walk for each boat to pass. Not to mention the time it took to raise or lower the water in the forty-nine locks.

Over the years, through the importance of the railroad and the improper maintenance of the Chemung Canal, it closed in 1878. Curious adventurers can easily find evidence of the Chemung Canal. Sections remain in Elmira in the swampy area east of Eldridge Park. You can follow the path north as it meanders just to the west of Lake Road. There are basins remaining in the area behind the Conifer Village apartments in Horseheads. It can be seen here and there along Route 14, between Horseheads and Montour Falls.

For more information, please refer to Gary Emerson's comprehensive history of the canal, *A Link in the Great Chain*, available at the Chemung County Historical Society, or at your local library.

Beginnings of the Elmira Police Department

By James Hare

There was no gunfight at the OK Corral, but there was a near riot on Water Street that developed after a Michigan cavalry regiment tried to "paint the town red". Shots were fired, one rioter was killed, two wounded and a reservist lost an arm attempting to restore order. In the mid 1860's, Elmira was a rough place.

An illustration of Dan Noble, a 19th century English gentleman burglar, from "Recollections of a New York Chief of Police" (1887) by George W. Walling. https://tinyurl.com/ydbn7g72

Historian Ausburn Towner wrote that it was a "period of uncomfortable doings." There was a "well organized gang of thieves and counterfeiters" who used Elmira as a rendezvous. Their chief occupation was stealing horses. Dan Noble, an English gentleman, burglar, confidence man, sneak thief and pickpocket plied his trade in the newly chartered city.

When Elmira became a city on April 7, 1864 it was protected by a skeleton force of men. There was a City Marshal (police chief), two special constables, two police constables and four night watchmen. Police work was no picnic. With no telephones, messengers were used to report trouble. If a prisoner could not walk to the lockup, he had to be carried, put in a wheel barrow, hand cart or passing wagon. Prisoners who put up resistance were clubbed into submission, with the policeman often receiving the worst of the fight.

Law enforcement was an important issue in the city election of 1865 (one year terms at that time). The Elmira *Advertiser* claimed, "the amount of crime committed in this city is great... the fact that it is a military post adds to the labors of the Recorder (city judge). The large amount of money disbursed here by the government has drawn here great numbers of criminals to gobble it up...." "Scrimmages" were occurring between patrol guards and disorderly soldiers. Because of the "frequency of the affrays and assaults" nightly occurring about the city, limiting the sale of intoxicating liquor was advocated.

With the election of Mayor John I. Nicks in 1865, a new City Marshal, John Stewart Knapp was appointed. As special constable (detective) he had broken up the gang of thieves and he would eventually become Elmira's first police chief when the Police Commission was formed in 1876. Between 1865 and 1876 politics affected the police. It was accepted practice to appoint the Watchmen (police officers) based on service to the party then in power and generally in particular wards. During that period Elmira had six changes in the position of chief with one year having co-chiefs.

Steps were taken to at least get the police properly dressed. In March of 1865, the Common Council authorized the, "City Marshal and subordinate officers shall wear uniforms while on duty and such uniforms shall be designated by the Mayor." In May, Mayor Nicks requested the support of voters for a special tax, $8,000 of which was for "police purposes." He said, "we all know the importance of an efficient Police and to have them efficient we must have good men and must pay them for their services..." The city would no longer depend on a volunteer police force.

On June 7, 1865 the newspaper reported, "The Night Police donned their new uniforms last evening for the first time. The material is dark blue, broad cloth made in England expressly for the wear of police..." The department was taking shape.

Elmira Celebrates the Fourth

by Diane Janowski

In 1906, Peter Schornsteimer had a grocery store on Lake Street. Friends and patrons gathered there every evening for lively discussion. This fun-loving group called themselves the "Senators." They planned a huge Fourth of July celebration and collected money for expenses.

Under a beautiful blue sky, the festivities began at 2:00pm at the corner of Lake and East Clinton Streets next to the Elmira Free Academy. Hager's Band played patriotic marches and popular songs for the 15,000 happy Elmirans who came to celebrate.

At 3:30pm the athletic events began with a 100-yard dash down the middle of Clinton Street, followed by a greased pole with a $5 bill at the top for the first to reach it, a pie eating contest, a greased pig chase, a wheelbarrow race, a sack race, a 3-legged race, and a potato race. Tut Payne reached the $5 bill first, and a proud youngster named Jones caught (and kept) the slippery pig. The Senators ended the evening with a banquet at William Maurer's saloon at 119 Lake Street.

July 4, 1931, in the darkest year of the Depression, Elmirans celebrated on a grand scale. It had been a hot week, and Brand Park Pool was the place to cool off. It was so hot that staffers at the *Star-Gazette* fried eggs on the sidewalk during their coffee breaks.

Elmira City Recreation director Joseph Riley planned programs at all our city parks. Every park had a "freckle contest" with prizes for children for the biggest or the most freckles. Track and field events had 3,000 young participants with many prizes.

At Eldridge Park, Mrs. Mable Anthony of Columbia Street hollered her husband's name, "P-h-i-l-e-t-u-s!" and won the husband calling contest. In the husband beating contest (using a dummy husband, but a real rolling pin), Mrs. Genevieve O'Leary, also of Columbia Street won first prize for her accuracy and enthusiasm. Eldridge Park held a watermelon-eating contest.

Rin Tin Tin, "The Wonder Dog of Stage and Screen" was live and in person at the Keeney Theater doing his vaudeville act. Councilman John Sheehe of the Eastside took all the children in his district to see the wondrous dog. Rinnie provided "autographed" photographs to the first 500 in line.

Our hospitals reported fourteen injuries related to the celebration, including six fireworks-related injuries. A man on Tuttle Avenue shot off his hand with a revolver while celebrating the holiday.

On July 4, 1954 at Eldridge Park, the big show was "Naitto's Dogs – Canine Acrobats." The Melody Garden Restaurant near Eldridge Park served clam chowder to Elmirans who came to hear the Merrymakers. Waverly hosted a big rodeo at Memorial Stadium. Movies playing that day were "Skirts Ahoy" at the Elmira Drive-In, and "How To Marry a Millionaire" at the New Heights theater. Shangri-La Speedway in Owego advertised a 100-mile race. Many people with cars drove to Ithaca to see fireworks.

July 4, 1972 was not much of a day for celebrating in Elmira. Less than two weeks after the Agnes flood, most Elmirans spent the day cleaning flood debris from their homes and yards. Telephone, gas, and postal service had not yet been restored. City water was undrinkable, and many were without electricity. Eldridge Park was closed and still a mess. Dunn Field and Brand Park pool were not yet repaired. Harris Hill park was open. There were no fireworks because Elmira was under curfew at night.

July 4, 1990 was very hot with temperatures in the 90s. Elmira had spectacular fireworks near the Madison Avenue bridge with thousands of spectators. Hill's Department Store had its own fireworks show. Even the Mark Twain Drama celebrated the Fourth (although on July 3) with a big fireworks display.

Championship of the Universe

by James Hare

Lincoln Beachey (in plane) racing against Barney Oldfield (in automobile). Image courtesy of United States Library of Congress's Prints and Photographs division.

Glenn Curtiss acknowledged in the Elmira *Star-Gazette* on July 19, 1911 that Lincoln Beachey was the "most reckless, daring and skillful air navigator of the present day..." He had recently flown over Niagara Falls, driving through the spray, going under the suspension bridge and down the gorge. Beachey, the barnstorming "Master Birdman," was to appear July 26th and 27th at the Maple Avenue Driving Park in an event sponsored by the Elmira *Star-Gazette*. Curtiss would have personal charge and supervision of the exhibition.

In 1886, the Maple Avenue Athletic Association was formed on lands owned by the Robinson family (in the vicinity of the present day Dunn Field). They laid out a half mile horse track with a baseball diamond and football field at the center. In 1889, the "Interstate Fair Association" was formed and added an elaborate grandstand, clubhouse, barns and a display building. Around the turn of the century the property passed into the hands of the Elmira Water, Light and Railroad Company. They established the first electric street cars to the field from Lake and Market Streets. The first night football game was played there in 1902. Eventually it would be renamed Recreation Park and in 1939 became Dunn Field.

Barnstorming was a great attraction. Just a few days before Beachey's arrival in Elmira, the Elmira *Advertiser* sponsored an Aviation Meet at the Chemung County Fair Grounds. That event featured René Simon, "the Fool Flyer," doing his reckless "Dip of Death" and Rene Barrier, "the Cloud Chaser," together known as the Moisant International Aviators. Simon said of Beachey, "*he iss better zan all of zem.*"

The Maple Avenue event had a number of special features. The *Gazette* posed the question "who wants to fly in an aeroplane?" All Elmirans were eligible, they just needed to be nominated on the form that was in the paper. Two people would get to fly with Beachey. Beachey would also present a "vivid" illustration of the value of the aeroplane in warfare. "Armed with imitation bombs the aviator will sail into the air and proceed to attack the imaginary enemy" which would be a large target in front of the grandstand.

A surprise emerged when Asa W. LaFrance, President of the LaFrance Motor Car Company, challenged Beachey to a race between his Curtiss bi-plane and La France's Chalmers Forty automobile. Beachey accepted stating, "the faster the motor car can go the better I will like it for there is nothing quite so fascinating to me as speed."

Beachey's plane was shipped to Elmira in sections to be assembled before the flight. On the first day of the event an estimated 10,000 people crowded the park. Charles Teasdale (1,401 votes) and Edward Loop (1,238 votes) were the winners of the popularity contest to fly with Beachey. Prior to the event Beachey mingled unrecognized in the crowd looking at his plane in the midst of a downpour.

The program consisted of four flights: distance, dips and glides, altitude and finally the race. Despite the rain, on the first flight Beachey flew towards Wellsburg, then banked over Sullivan's Monument disappearing behind the hills, then emerged over the city circling the *Star-Gazette* building three times. He flew eighteen miles in eighteen minutes. During the second flight he dipped at the grand stand "causing women to scream" ending with his famous special glide. *Star-Gazette* postcards were dropped on the first flight and popcorn bombs on the second.

The highlight was the race. The Chalmers Forty, driven by George Saulsman, was capable of 70 miles per hour. The race would be 2½ miles or five times around the track. Operated skillfully, the car was "puffing and snorting". The "curves offered little hindrance to the daring driver who assisted by allowing his body to hang out over the running board to prevent skidding at the turns." On the back stretch Beachey thrilled the crowd by swooping down over the car so that the two machines were running one directly over the other at a speed of 70 miles per hour. The plane won.

Three years later, in 1914, Beachey would return to Elmira to race Barney Oldfield. It would be labeled "The Dare Devil of the Ground verses The Demon of the Skies for the Championship of the Universe." Oldfield, at Indianapolis in 1903, had been the first man to accomplish a mile-a-minute performance. Once again the crowd was huge. One policeman counted 927 cars going through the gate and commented that he "never knew there were so many automobiles."

Oldfield used a 300-horsepower Christie racing automobile against Beachey's specially constructed aeroplane with an 80 horsepower Gnome motor called the "Little Looper." Throttles were open, Oldfield had to swerve his car tilting on two wheels to miss an old man with a cane, the woman next to him fainted, there were clouds of dust and unmuffled engines. Once again Beachey flew directly over the car with wheels almost touching Oldfield's head. The plane won.

"You do not often strike bad roads up in the air do you Mr. Beachey," asked an enthusiastic automobile owner. Beachey smiled, "no there are no real bumps up there but you may be surprised when I tell you I am thrown out of my seat while thousands of feet up in the air... I cannot say it is a pleasant sensation."

COMPETITIVE DESIGN FOR
CITY HALL

PERSPECTIVE VIEW
FROM SOUTH EAST

PIERCE & BICKFORD
ARCHITECTS

The prize winning architectural drawing by Pierce & Bickford, architects, for the new Elmira City Hall in 1895. Image courtesy of the Barnes Library.

Our City Hall

by Diane Janowski

I n January 1793, Newtown (now known as Elmira) built a "justice building" as a seat of regional government as required by Tioga County (now Chemung County). They built a two-story log cabin on the corner of Sullivan and East Church Streets that housed a jail and a home for the sheriff on the first floor. A room for holding court or public worship was on the second floor. Behind the cabin was a small cemetery. This building served the county for nearly thirty years.

In 1824, the cabin was abandoned, and a new county courthouse was built on Lake Street. This building was moved in 1862 to Market Street between Lake and Baldwin Streets and became Elmira's first City Hall. In its place on Lake Street the present Chemung County courthouse was erected.

A new Elmira City Hall became necessary. Elmira held a contest for the design of a suitable municipal building "[its construction] costs not to exceed $68,000." A committee of alderman chose Joseph Pierce and H. H. Bickford's design and awarded them the $100 prize. The committee had the power to alter to Pierce & Bickford's design to keep the cost within the budget.

Elmira City Hall was erected in 1895 for $118,000 in the Beaux-Arts style. Terra cotta embellishment at the capitals, belt courses, and pediments adorn the façade. Bas-reliefs and figural sculptures are incorporated. The arched front doors make a grand entrance that lead to a noble staircase.

As regional architects, Pierce & Bickford shaped the character of Elmira between 1885 and 1925 in their legacy of designing several hundred buildings. Their designs exemplified and promoted then-popular styles of architecture.

A terrible fire destroyed the top floor of Elmira City Hall on November 18, 1909, caused by a defective electric wire in the City Engineer's room near the roof. The loss was estimated at $50,000. The clock tower and the roof collapsed onto the third floor. The inferno devastated the council chambers and the city lost valuable records.

This building also houses the Elmira City Jail. Daring escapes occurred early in the 20th century. In 1905, prisoner Mary Donahue escaped the grasp of the police matron, Mrs. Mary Bruner, and climbed out onto the narrow ledge just below the second story windows. She scaled around the building, found an open window, climbed back in, jumped to the first floor landing and walked out the front door. On May 22, 1906, prisoner George Magee, while housed in the basement jail for crimes committed during his impersonation of a psychic, sawed through five steel bars in less than 10 minutes and escaped.

Elmira City Hall is located in the "Civic Historic District." This district holds the largest concentration of Elmira's significant historical architecture, including the six county buildings, City Hall, the Federal building, the former YMCA, the Chamber of Commerce (erected as the Steele Memorial Library), the Arnot Art Museum, and the Chemung County Historical Society.

Next time you're at the corner of East Church and Lake Streets, look up to the top of our City Hall – you'll see Native Americans, a farmer plowing a field, a locomotive, Hermes – the goddess of commerce, an easel, sculptors' tools, and an eagle.

Elmira Declares War on Tuberculosis

By James Hare

Postcard view of the hospital. Publisher: Baker Bros.

Sometimes known as the "Captain of Death, white plague, wasting disease, consumption, the fight against tuberculosis was the "first public health campaign in American History." On November 21, 1908, the *Star-Gazette* announced the city's declaration of war coming "from the most representative body of citizens that has assembled in a long time." Former mayor, Zebulon R. Brockway was made "commander in chief" with a staff that included Congressman J. Sloat Fassett and Mayor Daniel Sheehan.

The forum for announcing the campaign against TB was the Conference of Charities and Corrections which was held that November in the newly constructed Federation Building in Elmira. Several hundred delegates from across the state attended, breaking the previous record. Leading authorities pointed out that, "blindness in children may be prevented," and that alcohol was "a poison and menace to humanity." Other topics included "voluntary patients in state hospitals for the insane, the duty of the state to support the destitute and neglected children and employer's liability and worker's compensation."

A large map of the city had been made locating, with black pins, where deaths had occurred from tuberculosis since 1890. The feeling was this was the most "graphic way" to estimate the extent of the disease. It was estimated that 10% of the deaths in the city resulted from tuberculosis. Reports stated that the number of people in New York State suffering from tuberculosis was "equal to the combined populations of Poughkeepsie, Niagara Falls and Albany" and had cost the state, $120,000,000 per year. It was also reported that 200,000 people per year across the nation died from pulmonary tuberculosis.

John M. Connally, President of the Chamber of Commerce, spoke on "The Crusade Against Tuberculosis From A Business Man's Point Of View." "When a man of business is asked to handle a subject he generally starts at once with his pencil and makes figures... the method of estimating losses in dollars and cents caused from death by tuberculosis may seem unfeeling but it is an economic view and one which should appeal to our taxpayers and city officials." Connally proposed a state law making it compulsory for every city in the state to "erect, equip and maintain a hospital for the treatment of tuberculosis." He estimated the cost at $25,000 to build and $7,000 a year to maintain, costing the "small taxpayer assessed at $1000 per year" $1.60 per year or .03 per week. His figures were based on an estimated economic loss per death of $3225 computed by Dr. Herman M. Biggs former chief medical officer of New York City. Using Biggs' numbers and the 47 deaths in Elmira in 1907, Connally claimed the city lost $102,350 or enough to "erect an excellent hospital." He observed, "I assure you all that Elmira, a city whose women can stand on the streets and in two days tag passers-by out of $3000 for the Home for the Aged," can undertake the project.

Pulmonary Tuberculosis, "produces severe and unresolved coughing, night sweats and progressive weight loss. It can progress slowly...or it can be rapid... infection achieving fatality in a matter of weeks." In a paper at the Chemung County Historical Society, Dr. Swen Larson wrote, "treatment in the early days consisted of complete bed rest, isolation and good diet. Because of the infectious nature of the disease sanitarium care was very important so that the infected person could be isolated." On the other hand, in an advertisement, it was claimed that use of "Duffy's Pure Malt Whiskey" would cause consumptives to regain "vigor and strength...and be in better health than in years before taking it."

Good news was announced by Dr. A. W. Booth, a leader in the "war on tuberculosis" and chair of the committee to seek a hospital, in early December 1908. He stated that, "if the city would accept and maintain a properly situated and equipped hospital, two persons, a man and his wife, who live away from Elmira, but who are desirous of doing something that will benefit Elmira would offer as a gift the Elmira County Club building as a possible site."

The anonymous couple was Charles and Alice Spaulding Rapelyea, formerly of Elmira, who wanted to make the donation in honor of their late son Edward who had died of pneumonia at age 32 in 1908. The Country Club building was on upper Underwood Avenue. It had opened in 1898.

The *Star-Gazette* reported it was, "ideal in construction, location and water supply for a hospital for treatment of cases of advanced tuberculosis. Its size is sufficient for accommodating 15 to 25 patients. Its valuation is $12,000. That is building and not extensive grounds... it is elevated, has a fine southern exposure and the great wide verandas would make ideal resting places for the patients." The cost for treatment would be free unless one could afford to pay the $12 per week.

On December 15, 1908, the Common Council voted to maintain the hospital and accepted the offer made by the Rapelyeas. There were rumors of opposition in the Town of Elmira, "born of lack of familiarity with the subject," but on December 28th the Town Board, without a sign of opposition, unanimously approved the site. The City of Elmira accepted ownership on August 2, 1909, with the sanitarium opening shortly thereafter.

Fire would destroy the sanitarium in 1915. It had been urged on the County Board of Supervisors early on that they should "consider a county hospital which would obviate the necessity of sending patients... to the county poor house in Breesport... and all the towns in the county would benefit with the city." This early example of shared services would lead the county to appropriate $17,000 in 1917 towards the cost of a new sanitarium on the same site, and accept title from the city. The sanitarium would close in 1955.

From 1890-1907 there were 955 deaths in Elmira caused by tuberculosis. During the period 1895-1908 there were 1,564 cases of typhoid fever and 218 deaths. While the city was fighting tuberculosis, the matter of water purification was also an important struggle.

Explosions!

by Diane Janowski

BLAST KILLS THREE IN ELMIRA

Explosive Compound Goes Off in Factory Causing Death of Two Workmen and a Boy— Five Others Injured.

WHOLE CITY ROCKED BY TREMENDOUS SHOCK

Plant Literally Wiped Out by Explosion and Fire— No Explanation of Tragedy, and Those Who Could Tell Are Dead.

Front page on the Buffalo [New York] *Courier,* June 2, 1903

An explosion at the Chemung Canal Bank on East Water Street on Monday, October 20, 1884 caused great excitement. The gas was left turned on in the vault the Saturday before and the flame smothered itself out.

John Arnot, Jr., congressman and cashier at the bank, attempted to enter the vault Monday morning carrying a candle. The tremendous explosion blew him across the room against the cashier's counter. Arnot's whiskers and hair were completely burned off. Every window in the bank was blown out, the vault doors were twisted and the locks torn off. A great crowd gathered in the street. The Buffalo *Evening News* reported: "John Arnot Blown Up – The Millionaire Congressman Badly Injured by a Gas Explosion."

The Chemung Canal Bank eventually became the home of the Chemung Valley History Museum at 415 East Water Street. The vault where the explosion took place is part of the museum tour.

From the Elmira *Advertiser*, February 1900:

> *The police this morning received information that led them to believe that the disturbance last night was caused by fisherman using dynamite. Two men were seen on the ice prior to the explosion. The cause was determined the next day – a young man was experimenting with nitroglycerine."*

On June 1, 1903 at 5:10 in the afternoon, there was a terrible accident at William B. Pratt's Explosives Manufacturing Company. The factory was just south of the city line on Pennsylvania Avenue (near today's Elmira High School). Two young men and a boy were killed, and five more employees injured, when 1,500 pounds of Joveite exploded.

"Joveite, in its complete state, can only be exploded by means of a high grade percussion cap, and it therefore seems probable that some of the ingredients exploded during the process of mixing." [Elmira *Daily Gazette*]

Work at the plant had ended as usual at 5:00PM. Fifteen employees went home, and eight remained to do extra work. Two men were screening Joveite for an upcoming order when the blast occurred. The men were blown over the tops of trees and landed 400 feet away in an adjoining field. Their dismembered bodies were unrecognizable.

Every house in the neighborhood suffered broken windows. The blast shook the entire city of Elmira, breaking hundreds of windows in the Water Street shopping area, a mile and a half away. The Explosives Manufacturing Company was "wiped out of existence, as the ruins took fire and burned to a cinder." Leveled were the plant's six buildings. A huge cloud of smoke was visible for miles.

The coroner's report stated that the "accident was unavoidable and that Joveite is not a dangerous explosive." It was his impression that "some foreign explosive substance became mixed with the Joveite." Owner William B. Pratt said he would have the plant running again in a few days, but 100 neighbors signed a petition for Pratt to build elsewhere. Joveite was never produced on South Main Street again. Pratt continued to argue that Joveite was safe and did not cause the explosion. "Joveite is tranquil and patient. Nothing disturbs its even temper except a detonator. Even children can play with it."

In January 1904, city workers used Joveite to break up Chemung River ice near the mouth of Hoffman Creek. The plant moved to Middlesex, New Jersey and failed in 1906.

On January 2, 1936, the Elmira Savings Bank exploded supposedly by a gas leak. At the time, the bank was located on the south side of East Water Street, directly at the foot of Baldwin Street. The entire front and interior of the nearly-new, three-story building was blown out by the blast. It shattered all the windows at the Rathbun Hotel across the street and in most of the businesses within the block. The shock was felt six miles away in Horseheads.

The vaults were safe and the columns supporting the cornice were intact. It was feared that treasurer Michael Leahy was dead, but he had left the building about five minutes earlier. All currency and paper had been placed in the vault before Mr. Leahy left. Police suspected a gas leak, although Leahy said he did not notice an odor.

The New York Times reported on January 4 that the "gas theory [was] dropped... and a New York City bomb expert was called in to investigate."

Sources:
Buffalo *Evening News*, October 20, 1884
Corning *Journal*, June 3, 1903
Elmira *Advertiser*, February 1900
Elmira *Daily Gazette*, June 5, 1903
Niagara Falls *Gazette*, October 23, 1884
Pittsburgh *Press*, January 3, 1936

Elmirans Vote For Parks

by James Hare

When the decade of the 1880s opened, Elmira's Wisner Park was the only city park. By 1910, Glen Marston would write in "The American City" that Elmira was a "city of parks and progress," with eight city parks, having a combined area exceeding 100 acres. The seeds for this growth may well have come from the failure of the city to act when Dr. Edwin Eldridge died in 1876.

"View in the Eldridge Park" by J.H. Whitley, circa 1870. Image courtesy of New York Public Library's Digital Library under the digital ID G91F110_011F

The Elmira *Daily Advertiser* reported on May 19, 1886, "the election yesterday to determine whether or not the city should buy the Hoffman grove, to be used as a public park, was probably the most spirited special election ever held in Elmira."

Southsiders objected because they had not received "additional school accommodations." Northsiders pointed out they might still want them and want Miller's grove for a park. When the votes were counted 529 favored purchasing the grove (9½ acres for $17,150) with 366 opposed. The paper observed, "arguments did not count much, as the men usually voted first, and argued afterward."

Hoffman grove "was originally part of the farm of George W. Hoffman, who was born in Elmira on February 9, 1822 and for many years was
a farmer and a leader in the agricultural interests of the Chemung Valley
and New York State...."

In 1864, George's son William sold the park area to George S. Mc-
Cann. He would eventually offer the land to the city. Mayor Henry Flood
made the case that it was the only grove within city limits where Sunday
school and family picnics could be held. At that time it was a natural am-
phitheater where "thousands" had attended funeral services for President
Grant in 1885. The *Daily Advertiser* reminded Elmirans of their lost opportunity to acquire Eldridge Park noting that when Dr. Eldridge "went
the way of his fathers, the city was given the opportunity of purchasing the
park with all its improvements and decorations for a nominal sum; but
dilly-dallied so long in making up its parsimonious mind that the property
was sold to a business firm, despoiled of its beauty and turned into an un-
sightly lumber yard."

In 1889, a second chance to acquire Eldridge Park emerged. Labeled the "Eldridge Park scheme" by the Elmira *Weekly Advertiser,* a pro-
posal was made by Julia S. Reynolds, Dr. Eldridge's daughter, to sell what
was left of the park to the city for $68,000. Negotiations continued, how-
ever, resulting in a purchase price of $37,500. A special election was called
for July 2, 1889. The referendum included a vote for sewer repair ($60,000)
and street appropriations ($10,000) as well as the funds to purchase the
park. The *Daily Advertiser* reported that, "the sewer and street appropriations were lost sight of in the contest over the purchase of the park...the
polls had not been open very long before the fight waxed warm...two police
officers were kept busy keeping the would be voters in line."

Voting took place at City Hall on Market Street. The paper also
noted that, "a dozen or fifteen hacks were kept busy and the hackmen all
favored the park and many of them tendered their services without pay."
Election results were 950 for the purchase with 285 opposed. Streets and
sewers each had 1,059 favorable votes.

Elmira's third major park of the 1880s would eventually become
Brand Park. Riverside Park was privately developed by Colonel David C.

Robinson and opened to the public in 1888. Robinson, the son of former governor Lucius Robinson, "was involved in the development of the city: street railway system, the gas and water works." He would become mayor and acquire the Lyceum Theater in the 1890's. Prior to the opening he said, "I have laid out a public park in Southport (the area south of Lake Street Bridge had been called "South Port" from the time a ferry had opened at that location) and named it Riverside Park. There are about 35 acres of land in the park and I have already spent $8,000 or $9,000 in grading, filling and other work."

The June flood of 1889 spoiled the park, and it was not put in repair after that. John Brand Jr., who held a lease on some of the land on Maple Avenue belonging to the Mutual Life Insurance Company (which controlled land formerly owned by the Sly family) laid out a park there which became a favorite point of recreation for south siders. In 1901, Brand offered to deed to the city land owned by him if the city decided to purchase 23 acres of land from the Mutual Insurance Company for $16,000. The land owned by Brand was called the "Buttonwoods" after a large stand of buttonwood or sycamore trees with seeds that resembled buttons located between Maple Avenue and the Chemung River. The purchase would include Brand Park, Riverside Park and the land lying along the river dike connecting both. A special election was called for August 27, 1901.

There appeared to be opposition to the purchase. The *Daily Advertiser*, on the day before the vote observed, "there are some croakers in Elmira who are always crying that the city is dead as a door nail and can never be resuscitated."

The paper went on to say, "we want all the parks we can get." The day of the election ex-mayor Charles Davison was visible at the polls. The Elmira *Gazette* reported that "he stated that when Eldridge Park was purchased during his administration, the south siders had been promised the help of the north siders when they wanted a park. I am keeping my promise, said the ex-mayor." With only a 25% turnout of the voters, the purchase of the park passed 730 for to 130 against.

His Mother Called Him "Harry"

by Diane Janowski

Harold "Hal" Roach was an Elmira boy, born the son of Charles and Mabel Roach of Columbia Street on January 14, 1892. Although others called him "Hal," his mother called him "Harry." Young Hal's first job was as a newspaper deliverer. One of his customers lived at Quarry Farm - Samuel Clemens.

In several *Star-Gazette* interviews, Hal said his childhood in Elmira was a happy one. In one interview Hal said, "Elmira was a fine place for a boy to grow up." He recalled playing in Grove Park as a child. After his death in 1992, Elmira renamed the park pavilion in his honor.

Hal Roach (1892-1992) circa 1920.
Anonymous photographer.

Hal claimed to have "attended and been kicked out of almost every school in Elmira." St. Patrick's, Booth, and Elmira Free Academy schools officially claim him as a former student. He attended EFA for a short period, and played football on its team. After his EFA expulsion in 1908 at age 16, Hal's father "strongly suggested" that Hal leave home in hopes that "traveling would help him grow up."

Roach went as far from Elmira as he could - Alaska. He mined for gold and when that did not prove advantageous, he delivered mail for two years in "Uncle Sam's service" (in Alaska) riding a horse for long distances through the wilderness. After nearly losing one foot to frostbite, Hal decided upon a less strenuous job. While on vacation in Los Angeles, he happened to meet some people connected with the motion picture business, and because of his riding skills learned while delivering mail, he secured himself a job as an extra in a movie. As an extra, the director placed him in a gambling den scene. The director did not know the game nor did the other extras, but Hal did. Hal straightened out some details, and the director rewarded him a regular job.

Hal worked hard and finally became the assistant director. Eventually in 1915, he formed a company with Dan Linthicum. Dan supplied the money, while Hal supplied the brains. They took the first letters of their names, R-O-L-I-N, as their company name. The companies who bought their movies went broke and with Rolin's capital down to zero, Roach decided to risk it all on one last effort. Their next movie had no story, or "rhyme or reason." Hal called it "Just Nuts" with Harold Lloyd, and sent it to the Pathè Movie Company. Pathè bought it and asked for several more. Hal's company had more good players - including Harry Pollard, and Bebe Daniels.

Rolin had its own studio, several directors and all the money it needed. Hal worked hard for his success. Elmira's Regent Theater made famous his "Lonesome Luke" comedies locally.

Neither Mr. Roach bought nor wrote any scenario. He thought out comedy situations, outlined his ideas to his company, and put his crew to it. This method proved successful. According to IMDB, Hal produced 650 films in his lifetime.

In 1937, Mrs. Roach visited Elmira to renew acquaintances with her old friends. She told the Elmira *Star-Gazette* that since she moved to California in 1916, she had met Joan Crawford, Mary Pickford, Claudette Colbert, and Jean Harlow. Mrs. Roach said that she was proud of her son, and that she and her husband were reluctant to leave Elmira when Hal coaxed them to move to California "where there was real living." She said that she did not regret moving west although she missed her friends in Elmira. She lived at her son's studio in Culver City, California until her death. Hal died in 1992 at age 100, and was buried in Woodlawn Cemetery.

Sources:
Elmira *Advertiser*, September 15, 1916.
Elmira *Star-Gazette*, June 13, 1937.
Elmira *Star-Gazette*, January 12, 1992.
http://www.imdb.com/title/tt0005582/

Frank Gannett and the Birth of the Star-Gazette

by James Hare

Postcard view of the Elmira *Star-Gazette* building. Publisher Baker Bros.

rank Gannett reached the Elmira Star-Gazette office at seven in the morning and left at nine at night. Sundays, he dropped around to, "pick up the pieces." Upon arrival at the office for his fourteen hour day, he frugally changed his clothes, put on a pair of old trousers and well-worn shoes without laces. Then he sat down at the biggest piece of furniture in the news room, a roll-top desk as large as a Pullman upper birth, which it somewhat resembled. When the hands of the clock reached eight, it was his custom to look up and around the room. He was ready to hand out the day's assignments; and any reporter who stumbled in a few minutes after received this brisk uniform reminder: "Eight o'clock's the hour; eight o'clock's the hour!"

Next came the cry, "Copy! Copy! Copy!" Each piece of copy which the managing editor "edited and adorned with a headline he carried to the composing room himself. He did not walk, but ran, and sometimes his unlaced shoes went flying off his feet. Coming back he ran and plunked himself down at his desk, again repeating, Copy! Copy! Copy!"

- from the book *Imprint of a Publisher* by Samuel T. Williamson, 1948

One day in May of 1906, Frank Gannett ate lunch at the Langwell Hotel in Elmira while awaiting a change of trains on his trip from Pittsburgh to Ithaca. John Causer, the proprietor of the hotel, told him that, "a young fellow named Davenport, who had come to Elmira the year before and bought an interest in the *Gazette* needed a partner."

The *Gazette* was a "rabid Democratic afternoon rival of the *Evening Star*," a thinly disguised Republican paper. The third daily paper in Elmira at the time was the *Advertiser*, owned by Congressman J. Sloat Fassett and unabashedly Republican. Instead of traveling to Ithaca, Gannett met with Erwin R. Davenport, whom he had previously met in Ithaca. They agreed that they could make the Gazette a success if Gannett became a partner.

Frank Gannett was born September 15, 1876 on Gannett Hill overlooking Canandaigua Lake. At the age of one his family moved to Steuben County to a hamlet called Bloods Depot (Atlanta near North Cohocton). His family moved around the county to Howard, Wallace and Bolivar. Frank sold newspapers, saving what he could. Eventually he would attend Cornell University, editing the Cornell *Sun*, the campus newspaper. Upon graduation he would become city editor of the Ithaca *Daily* and had a brief run as editor of *Frank Leslie's Illustrated Weekly*, in New York City. Just prior to his visit in Elmira, he had been editing *The Index* in Pittsburgh, which in his words was "an unimportant little rag."

The *Gazette* had been founded in 1828. The first newspaper in Chemung County was the *Telegraph* first published in December of 1815. "It was a small sheet, a page of which was 12 by 20 inches in size and four columns in width." Under new ownership the paper became the Newtown *Telegraph* and a rival newspaper appeared named the *Vedette* in 1818. Both papers were discontinued and *The Investigator* began in 1819, with Job A. Smith as the printer. In 1822, *The Investigator* became the Tioga *Register* and in August of 1828 became the Elmira *Gazette* under the control of Job A. Smith. (the same year the Village of Newtown was renamed Elmira) The *Gazette* was a weekly paper until 1856 when it became a daily for half a year. In 1860, it returned to being a daily on a permanent basis.

Purchasing a half interest in the *Gazette* was a challenge for Gannett. He soon learned that Davenport's partner, Royal Soper, was a front for David B. Hill, the real owner. Hill was a former Elmira Mayor, New York Governor and United States Senator whose political creed was "I am a Democrat." By 1906, Hill had retired from politics and lived near Albany at his country home Wolfert's Roost. He had a "dominating personality." Gannett was going on thirty and there was "nothing high pressure" in him. Gannett spent three days with Hill before Hill asked for $20,000 for his half interest. That was "nearly seven times the young editor's savings." Davenport had paid the same price for his half interest. Gannett had $3,000 in savings, he raised an additional $7,000 on "character credit" and Hill accepted $10,000 in personal notes. Years later Gannett said, "I am frequently asked how I became a newspaper owner. The only way is to save your money and at the same time establish credit."

When Gannett took over his half interest, it was agreed that he would handle news and editorials while Davenport continued running the business end. The paper's capacity was eight pages. The *Gazette* remained the spokesman of the Democratic Party, it "exchanged punches" with the Republican *Advertiser* while the *Evening Star* was its' rival in news and circulation. The "*Gazette* was beset by two enemies. The *Advertiser* struck at its mouth and the *Evening Star* at its stomach."

The *Evening Star* was owned by two brothers-in-law, Isaac Seymour Copeland and James F. Woodford, both approaching retirement age. The paper was first published on May 24, 1888 as a penny paper. Copeland's son, Woodford J. Copeland, an eye, ear, nose, and throat physician was the editor. The *Star* was over subscribed for its advertising rates and with the *Gazette* buying a new press merger talks began. Dr. Copeland and Gannett agreed that Elmira could only support one afternoon daily. They agreed to merge and a new daily, the Elmira *Star-Gazette* was first published on July 1, 1907 at 2 cents per copy.

This was the beginning of the Gannett media empire. In 1912, Gannett personally purchased the Ithaca *Journal* and merged it with the Ithaca *News* creating the *Journal News*. In 1916, Gannett, Davenport, and Dr. Copeland with money which they said they "begged, borrowed and stole," bought the Rochester *Times* and the Rochester *Union & Advertiser* and created the Rochester *Times Union*. In 1918 Gannett relocated to Rochester to manage that paper. In 1921, they took over two Utica papers founding the Utica *Observer Dispatch*.

Closer to home, 1923, was the year that the *Advertiser* (founded in 1853 as Fairman's *Daily Advertiser* becoming the *Advertiser* in 1854 with a subscription rate of $4.00 per year) and the *Sunday Telegram* (founded in 1879 for a startup price of $75) were purchased by Elmira *Star-Gazette*, Inc. Dr. Copeland became the publisher of the Elmira papers and Frank Tripp became the manager.

In 1924, Erwin Davenport and Dr. Copeland decided to retire. Gannett bought their interests making him the principal owner of all the properties. Frank Tripp, who had been a reporter and had purchased James F. Woodford's interest, became general manager of all the Gannett Newspapers.

It's on the Books

by Diane Janowski

Laws are very important to the citizens of a town. Actual laws and resolutions taken from the Village of Elmira's Board of Trustees' meetings from 1831 to 1849.

July 25, 1831
No person shall have any slaughterhouse within the limits of the Village of Elmira unless he has gotten a license in writing signed by the Trustees.

May 9, 1835
The street running along the bank of the Chemung River through said Village shall be denominated "River Street."

July 19, 1836
Resolved, that the Board of Trustees, hereafter, holds its meetings at the Eagle Tavern.

May 5, 1841
The following petition was presented:

> "To the Trustees of the Village of Elmira, Gentlemen, Mr. Frederick Granger and I join lots in the upper part of this Village, his line is within a few feet of my house on the corner of his lot, and immediately on the line and within five or six feet of the door of my house he has erected a cow shed and a hog pen which is very offensive and dangerous to the health of my family. I hereby apply to you the said Trustees to abate the said nuisance. I refer to you the 15th Ordinance of Chapter 1 of the Laws & Ordinances of the Village of Elmira.

signed - Asa Blivens

The eastern side of Wisner Park when it was a cemetery, circa 1855.

November 4, 1841
The report of the Chief Engineer was presented and which recommends supplying the Engine with 200 feet of hose. The hose to be gotten from New York.

July 20, 1843
Resolved, that notice will be given to John Arnot to fix his sidewalk in 20 days and that his stoop will be removed or it will be done for him.

June 5, 1844
Resolved, that the bridge of the Canal on Water Street is unsafe and highly dangerous to the traveling public who are compelled to cross it, and request the immediate attention of the State Authorities.

September 24, 1846
Resolved, that the Public Square will be enclosed with a rough board fence.

May 4, 1847
Resolved, that the Board will buy 60 forest trees and materials needed for setting out said number of trees in the Public Square and Graveyard of this Village.

June 25, 1849
On Motion, resolved that one dozen catallpah (sic) trees will be gotten from Rochester next Fall for the public square and the Court House yard.

Helen Keller: Mark Twain and Elmira

by James Hare

> *"I am filled with the wonder of her knowledge,*
> *acquired because shut out from all distractions.*
> *If I could have been deaf, dumb and blind, I*
> *also might have arrived at something."*
>
> Mark Twain Speeches

> *"Blindness is an exciting business, I tell you;*
> *if you don't believe it get up some dark night*
> *on the wrong side of your bed, when the house is*
> *on fire and try to find the door."*

- Helen Keller from her book *Midstream*

Helen Keller first met Samuel Clemens (Mark Twain) at the age of fourteen, in March of 1895, at a luncheon held in her honor by Laurence Hutton, an editor, critic and friend of Twain. Keller and Twain were immediately drawn to each other. She said, "he entered into my limited world with enthusiasm just as he might have explored Mars. Blindness was an adventure that kindled his curiosity. He treated me not as a freak, but as a handicapped woman seeking a way to circumvent extraordinary difficulties." Hutton observed that, "he was peculiarly tender and lovely with her - even for Mr. Clemens - and she kissed him when he said goodbye."

Clemens was so impressed that he persuaded his good friend Henry Rogers of Standard Oil to manage Helen's finances to support her education. Rogers was doing the same for the bankrupt Twain. Rogers work made it possible for Keller to attend Radcliffe from which she graduated *cum laude*.

In a letter written March 29, 1895 Helen wrote, "I think Mark Twain is a very appropriate *nom de plume* for Mr. Clemens because it has a funny and quaint sound that goes well with his amusing writings, and its nautical significance suggests the deep and beautiful things he has written." Writing to Twain, after the death of his wife in 1904, she wrote, "...

Helen Keller. Image courtesy of Library of Congress. digital ID cph.3c12513.

do try to reach through grief and feel the pressure of her hand, as I reach through darkness and feel the smile on my friends lips and the light in their eyes, though mine are closed."

Mark Twain wrote in his autobiography of the challenge he faced in 1906, when he chaired the first meeting of the Association to assist the blind when he had to read a letter from Helen who was sick and could not attend.

The letter made Twain emotional and he introduced it saying, "if I knew anything about literature, here was a fine, and great, and noble example of it..." He wrote later that, "she will be as famous a thousand years from now as she is today." Helen and Anne Sullivan Macy visited Twain at Stormfield, his home in Connecticut, in 1909. While there, he read to her from "Eve's Diary" concluding with "wherever she was, there was Eden"(his tribute to his late wife Livy). When Helen signed the guestbook at the end of her visit, she wrote, "I have been in Eden three days and saw a King. I knew he was a King the minute I touched him though I had never touched a King before."

Mark Twain recognized the contribution of Anne Sullivan Macy who had worked with Helen from age seven and brought her to life. He gave Anne a souvenir of her Stormfield visit in the form of a postcard on which he wrote, "To Mrs. Anne Sullivan Macy with warm regard & limitless admiration of the wonder she has performed as a "miracle-worker." This description, coined by Twain, would become the title of the movie by the same name about Anne Sullivan and Helen Keller.

The Elmira *Advertiser* reported on April 19, 1926 "Helen Keller is looking forward to her visit to Elmira for she has been informed Mayor David N. Heller is planning a real welcome for her." She was coming to Elmira on behalf of the American Foundation for the Blind and would speak at two events. She would appear at the Majestic Theater at 3PM and at The Park

Church at 7:30 PM, Sunday, April 25th.

Frederic H. Hill, honorary chairman of the event stated that, "Elmira cannot make too much of the visit...her coming to Elmira should arouse a two-fold interest. One in herself, because she is a remarkable woman; the other because of the spirit which brings her here—a spirit of service to others who are suffering as she, in order that what she has done for herself may be within the reach of them also."

Miss Keller arrived Thursday, April 22nd, checking into the Langwell Hotel. That evening she was off to Canandaigua to speak and the next night traveled to Penn Yan. Her entourage included Anne Sullivan Macy, who would speak of her association with Helen and Edwin Grasse, a blind musician and composer. He could play the violin, piano and organ. The *Advertiser* noted that, "traveling about as he does, with Miss Keller, Mr. Grasse has to memorize the stops of a different organ every night for he seldom finds two organs alike."

The newspapers reported Helen Keller's remarks at the Park Church, "I have come the long, dark way all the blind must go, and I know from experience the difficulties they encounter. I once was alone in the world because no one could communicate with me, not even my dear mother. Then my teacher came, and with a little word dropped from her fingers a ray of light from her soul, touched the darkness of my mind, and I awoke to the sunshine and beauty of the world. It is because somebody cared about me, and helped me to overcome my limitations that today I am a reasonably happy and useful human being. If you care, if we can make the people of this country care, the blind will triumph over blindness..."

The *Star-Gazette* reported, "there was light even in the darkness; understanding even in the soundlessness as Helen Keller addressed two capacity audiences Sunday in Elmira... she told the simple unaffected story, now and then breaking into laughter for the sheer joy of being able to speak so that Elmira could hear her."

(a special note on sources: the information about Mark Twain and Helen Keller was from Twain & Keller A Special Relationship from the Mark Twain Library: October thru November 2012.)

Elmira's Junction Canal

by Diane Janowski

Most Elmirans know the story of the Chemung Canal, but many have not heard of the Junction Canal. The Chemung Canal served as an efficient solution to transport goods and raw materials to and from the Erie Canal and the Southern Tier from 1833 to 1878. In the city of Elmira, the Chemung Canal approximately followed the route of the Clemens Center Parkway.

By 1839, enterprising businessmen of Chemung County solicited the New York State Legislature to undertake the making of a connection from the Chemung Canal to the North Branch Canal at Athens, Pennsylvania. It was argued that "thousands of tons of coal would be brought over this route from the great anthracite coal region of the Susquehanna to supply the cities, the flourishing villages and the salt works of New York, and that there would be an extensive interchange of commodities between the citizens of those States."

In 1846, the Junction Canal Company was incorporated. Its President and chief stockholder was John Arnot, who had investments in many Pennsylvania coalmines. Ground was broken in 1853 and the main portion was finished in 1854.

The waterway cut off from the Chemung Canal at the steel rolling mills, near today's East Washington Avenue and Clemens Center Parkway. It extended east, twisting and turning through Elmira's Eastside. It traveled along the north side of the Chemung River, sometimes actually in the river, for a distance of eighteen miles to the State line. Aqueducts were built to pass over Newtown Creek, Baldwin Creek and Wyncoop Creek. There were eleven locks and three dams, the latter used as feeders to replenish the water supply.

It was not until 1858 that the Junction Canal Company had its line throughout in operation. The size of the canal, according to a report of the company to the Pennsylvania authorities in 1867, was sixty-five feet

Corning Journal.

CORNING. N. Y.

THURSDAY, APRIL, 30, 1868.

☞ The Canals of the State are to be opened Monday, May 4th. The Chemung Canal and Feeder will be in readiness. The Elmira *Advertiser* states that the Junction Canal will not be ready until May 20th, as a dam at Chemung, was partially destroyed in a recent freshet.

From the Corning (New York) *Journal,* April 30, 1868.

at water line, twenty-six feet at bottom, and four-feet in depth. The cost of construction was reported as $530,637.

The route was in use for about thirteen years after its entire completion, during which time it was an important tributary to the New York State canals, and the company received gratifying returns. In 1866, the name of the company was changed to the Junction Canal and Railroad Company, and the officials were authorized to construct a railway if they so desired.

It was not a coincidence that John Arnot built his gas works on Madison Avenue right on the edge of the Junction Canal's William Street basin.

Regional railroads gradually absorbed the transportation of coal and other products. Traffic on the terminal canals diminished. In 1865, flooding caused the destruction of the North Branch canal in Pennsylvania. Traffic was supplemented by a railroad built along that canal route.

William Jeffers Saw and Planing Mill on William Street was erected around 1855. Its log yard with logs cut from Chemung County forests was piled high as far as the Lackawanna tracks and Madison Avenue. After the canal boat service was abandoned, the logs were floated in the old canal to the basin and hauled into the mill, where they were sawed and worked into finished lumber. Today it is the location of I.D. Booth, DeMuth Electric, and Spiegel's.

Unlike the Cayuga and Seneca, and the Oneida Lake canals, which, after being built and operated for a while by private companies, soon passed into the hands of the State, the Junction canal was under the management of an incorporated company during its entire existence.

Ice and flooding were the two major enemies of the canal system. The St. Patrick's Day flood of 1865 damaged the Junction Canal. Historian William Markham recalled in his 1869 "The Junction Canal" that in the town of Chemung in a single day he saw ninety boats go through its lock. The Junction Canal was operated for a part of the season in the autumn of 1871, and was then closed and abandoned.

Sources:

"Fire Breaks Out..." Elmira *Star-Gazette* April 30, 1908 page 2

http://en.wikipedia.org/wiki/Junction_Canal

http://www.americancanals.org/Data_Sheets/New%20York/
Junction%20Canal%20(NY).pdf

http://www.eriecanal.org/texts/Whitford/1906/Chap21.html
Towner, Ausburn History of Chemung County 1892

Markham, William "The Junction Canal" 1869

Whitford, Noble E.: *History of the Canal System of the State of New York, Vol. II*, Brandow
Printing Co., Albany, 1906

The Victory Arch at Wisner Park

By Diane Janowski

VICTORY ARCH AND MAIN STREET, ELMIRA, N. Y.

The Victory Arch across North Main Street postcard view.

On March 6, 1919 the Cunard liner Mauritania docked at Pier 56 at the foot of West 14th Street in New York City. It brought back from France Elmira's soldiers of Company L 108th Infantry 27th Division. Many civilian Elmirans had gone down to meet the ship. On board a special tugboat that greeted the Mauritania in the Atlantic Ocean, they held a banner with the words "Elmira Welcomes You Home."

Not everyone came back. Company L had lost 15 men killed in action, 1 missing, 2 dead in accidents, 1 died from illness. Company L stayed in New York City for its big welcome home parade on the 27th, and came home to Elmira the next day.

Back home in Elmira, Mayor Harry Hoffman's crew planned a grand parade and banquet at the Armory. Donations from citizens poured in. The committee decided to build a "semi-permanent" arch over North Main Street at Wisner Park, made of cement over a steel skeleton. One side read "Welcome and Honor Soldiers & Sailors" and the other "Chemung County Honors Her Heroes." It did have electricity so that you could see it at night. According to the *Star-Gazette* on April 1, it was "constructed in record-breaking time" during a terrible blizzard. It was meant to be temporary – "the span will remain for many months to be used on other occasions."

On March 28, factories, schools, and businesses closed early at 2:30pm to let everyone join the downtown activities. Fire bells and factory whistles blew at 3pm to signal people to get themselves downtown. Suburban trolleys brought hundreds of visitors earlier in the afternoon. Veterans of the Spanish-American War and the Civil War congregated at the Armory. "Handsomely decorated" automobiles provided by the Elmira Automobile Club lined up at City Hall for the mayor and aldermen. Daniel Livens donated his entire fleet of taxicabs for veterans who were unable to march. Many other private cars were also donated.

The special train #3 was to arrive at our Lackawanna station at 4:38pm. According to the *Star-Gazette* article on April 2, "the scene when the train pulled in bearing the Elmira members of Company L was impressive in the extreme." There was no great noise, no cheering or flag-waving. The great crowd was simply there to show how happy it was over the return of its soldier heroes. The crowd yelled the names of the soldiers as they exited the cars. The soldiers quickly mixed into the crowd and it was difficult to get them back into parade mode.

The formation of the parade began at the Lackawanna station (near today's Big Lots store). A platoon of policemen lead the parade, followed by the mayor and the Welcoming Committee. Then came Company L, the veterans of other wars, and the Boy Scout Bugle Corps. The veterans and the citizens marched through the streets. Leading the procession were automobiles carrying the mayor, the aldermen, and members of the Welcome Committee. The crowd moved faster than the parade so that they might see the soldiers march under the arch. The soldiers marched in "apparent indifference to the personal greetings of the crowds lining the sidewalks. They were solemn and unemotional. They looked neither to the right nor to the left with few exceptions."

The parade marched down Lake Street to East Water, turned right and proceeded to North Main Street. It turned north and walked under the Victory Arch. The police and Boy Scouts kept the streets clear and the crowds out of the way of the soldiers.

At Main and West Church Streets the parade ended. A silent ceremony honored those Elmirans who had died. The group then made its way to the Armory.

The large procession of men were met at the Armory, filled to its limit with mothers, wives, sweethearts, and sisters and finally broke rank. Companies were assembled in the drill hall for an address by Mayor Hoffman. He started by saying, "Boys, we're glad to see you." After the short address, friends and family of the soldiers rushed into the drill hall from the gallery above. After these festivities, fresh hot doughnuts and coffee was served for everyone at the Salvation Army at 155 Baldwin Street. Then everyone went home to their own receptions and parties. A banquet for the soldiers was held one week later at the Armory.

The city thought about taking the arch down as early as 1922. It lasted about ten more years with annual maintenance estimated at $2,500. The last mention I found of it in 1933 stated it was already gone.

Sources:

Elmira *Star-Gazette* "Shall city's Victory Arch be Razed?" January 18, 1922 Page 15
Elmira *Star-Gazette* "The Victory Arch" March 30, 1969 Page 7
Elmira *Star-Gazette* "Happy Days" March 7, 1919 page 6
Elmira *Star-Gazette* "Hello America! Hello Elmira!" March 7, 1919 page 11
Elmira *Star-Gazette* "Citizens Pay Tribute to Brave Heroes" April 1, 1919 page 7

Labor Day, 1903

by James Hare

FINE FEATURE OF LABOR DAY PARADE

G. H. COTTON, JR., & BRO. HAD FIF-TEEN CARTS AND TWENTY-NINE HORSES IN THE LINE MONDAY.

From the Elmira *Daily Gazette & Free Press*, September 9, 1903 page 7

"Most successful in every way was the celebration of Labor Day held in Elmira last Monday under the auspices of the Federation of Labor," according to the Elmira *Telegram* on September 13, 1903. The "celebration" was the joint labor demonstration of the entire Southern Tier organizations. The previous year it had been held in Binghamton and the 1904 "celebration" would be held in Ithaca.

The *Daily Gazette and Free Press* estimated that "twenty-five thousand strangers" visited Elmira on September 7th. "The Lackawanna Railroad ran three special trains to the city, each having twelve coaches loaded with visitors and every regular train was loaded. The Lehigh Valley had one train of twenty cars loaded with people from Ithaca. Residents from Addison, Sayre, Waverly, Corning, Hornellsville, Binghamton and intermediate points came to Elmira via the Erie." The Tioga ran an extra train for Morris Run, Lawrenceville and Arnot, Pennsylvania. The Northern Central and the trolley line brought the Watkins visitors.

Labor Day was a relatively new national holiday in 1903, having been declared that nine years earlier in 1894. It originated on "Tuesday", September 5, 1882 when approximately 10,000 workers marched in New York City from City Hall to Union Square and up to 42nd. Street. It was first proposed in May of that year under the auspices of an umbrella organization of 56 unions called the Central Labor Union, with the idea of building labor solidarity in the face of the changes brought by the Industrial Revolution.

Excitement in Elmira for the event began to build when it was announced on September 4th, after a midnight agreement, that the Father Mathew Temperance Society baseball team would play two games against the Kanaweola Cycle Club nine in Elmira on Labor Day.

The agreement was controversial because the Father Mathew team had previously agreed to play the White Ponies of Corning on that day. Elmira fans wanted to see the game and still participate in the big Labor Day demonstration, so "relations" with the White Ponies had to be broken.

The major event of the day would be the parade. It was described by the *Telegram* as a "monster." The crowd came early. "The marching organizations presented a fine appearance, many of them arrayed in garbs portraying their particular trade and they were repeatedly cheered along the line of the march." The Sayre painters brought along Hosmer's Marine Band, Geneva sent her, "painters, printers, metal polishers and carpenters." The little town of Valois sent her stone masons and the Valois Band. Corning contributed her butchers. The Cronk Hanger Band from Montour Falls, "whose showy uniforms of White Prince Albert coats, sky blue trousers and high bear skin caps made them a conspicuous feature of the parade."

One of the most interesting features of the parade was the display of G. H. Cotton Jr. and Brother, truck men. The display consisted of "fifteen conveyances" drawn by twenty-nine horses. One rig that drew special attention was the new forty-foot scenery truck which was for use at the local theater. The newspaper noted that the whole display represented a $12,000 investment.

Two local unions that were sparsely represented in the parade were the street car employees and the bartenders. Apparently they were needed elsewhere. It was reported that the "deportment" of the crowd was excellent. Few were observed in the streets as "under the influence." Those that did walk unsteady were of the "bummer class," and not members of labor unions.

The Grand Marshal was a well known labor leader Patrick H. Dowling with aides Edward W. Sweet and Michael H. O'Brian. In the van of the procession was a platoon of police officers commanded by Chief Cassada and assisted by Acting Captain Powell. The parade took an hour and fifteen minutes to pass a given point. It began on Lake Street heading to Water Street, Main Street, and West Third Streets, then countermarching to South Main Street, to West Henry Street, to Pennsylvania Avenue (Sly Street), to Maple Avenue, ending at the Maple Avenue Driving Park (currently the Dunn Field area).

At the park, addresses were given by R. M. Campbell of New York City, vice president of the Federation of Labor of New York. He spoke on the advantages and real purposes of organized labor. E. J. Lynch of Boston, president of the International Metal Polishers Association was the other speaker.

In addition to the baseball game and speeches a series of competitions took place. The 100- and 200-yard dashes were held. R.A. Miller was the only contestant who appeared for the motor cycle race.

"The greased pig provided great amusement being finally caught by a couple of youngsters who did good teamwork and who probably divided the porker," according to the *Daily Gazette and Free Press.*

To finish the day, Paine's Manhattan Beach fireworks were scheduled to put on a show, but rain began to fall in the late afternoon. Eventually the fireworks were postponed until September 17 when the "great display" would be given "with several additions."

A Big Explosion

By Diane Janowski

CAUSE IS A MYSTERY

Why the West Side Company's Boiler Exploded.

THUS TESTIFIED EXPERTS.

At the Inquest Held Last Evening—Frank
Albro Was a Thoroughly Competent
and Trustworthy Fireman—More
Frequent and Rigid Inspection
Recommended.

Elmira *Gazette & Free Press* April 7, 1897 page 8.

As someone who has researched local history for a long time can attest, weird phenomena come along. I discovered Elmira mentioned in a national publication for a huge story that received little or no recognition in our local papers.

The June 5, 1897 edition of *Scientific American* described a whopper of an explosion at the West Side Railroad's powerhouse on College Avenue that killed two employees. The magazine devoted one article and four large photos to the incident. It took me a while to find mention of it in our local papers.

Around 4:45AM on March 29, 1897, a loud explosion occurred and sent residents of northern Elmira to their windows. Many thought it was an earthquake, but the telltale plume of black smoke and flying debris proved otherwise.

The substantial brick building, located on College Avenue, north of Westside Avenue (the site of today's Hilliard Corporation), housed the engine and boiler room. Three locally-made Payne and Sons tubular boilers, and three Bates-Corliss engines were destroyed.

A horrible sight of confusion greeted the fire fighters who arrived at the scene. Bits and pieces of broken boilers, bricks, machinery, splintered timbers, sheets of tin, and trolley car parts were everywhere.

As there was no fire, the firemen quickly called the police department. A search for bodies found one dead, and one still alive. Engineer Philip Kaufelt was in the engine room when the explosion came. He was struck by timbers and thrown to the front of the room. He suffered a fractured skull and two broken legs. Someone took him to his home nearby. Hospital authorities quickly sent a nurse to attend to his situation. Night engineer Frank Albro was killed instantly, and found in a ghastly condition. Two other men in the building luckily made it out without injury.

When daylight arrived, it was evident that the explosion threw debris all over the property and neighborhood – some debris was found 500 feet away. According to the Owego *Gazette* on April 1, 1897, "The [West Side] building was wrecked and a portion of the boiler, weighing five or six tons, tore its way through two brick walls and two street cars, and was carried into a field, 180-feet distant, where it imbedded itself in the ground after having torn a ditch four feet wide and nearly two feet deep. The loss is about $30,000." The Ovid *Independent* April 6, 1897 stated, "the power house [was] a complete wreck."

Superintendent Jones put every available employee to work scouring the grounds for debris and clearing the trolley track, and getting the trolley cars out of the barn. As the West Side Railroad was incapable of producing electricity for their cars after the explosion, the Elmira and Horseheads Railroad allowed the West Side Railroad to tap into its electrical line with only a schedule delay of 2½ hours. Giving credit to the company for quick thinking after such a horrible morning, the West Side cars ran on time for the rest of the day.

The water gauge on one of the boilers may have been the culprit, but we will never know for sure. Engineer Philip Kaufelt died of his injuries four weeks later.

Sources:

"Peculiar Boiler Explosion," *Scientific American*, June 5, 1897. Vol. LXXVI. No. 23, page 357.

Elmira *Telegram*, Sunday, May 2, 1897

Elmira *Daily Gazette and Free Press*, March 30, 1897, page 3

Elmira *Daily Gazette and Free Press*, March 29, 1897, page 5.

Elmira *Daily Gazette and Free Press*, April 26, 1897, page 3

Owego *Gazette* on April 1, 1897, page 1

Ovid *Independent* April 6, 1897

1918 influenza poster courtesy Rensselaer County Tuberculosis
Association, Troy, N.Y.

Spanish Flu Epidemic of 1918

by James Hare

Adults wore masks while the children skipped rope to the rhyme:

> *I had a little bird*
> *Its name was Enza*
> *I opened a window*
> *And In-Flu-Enza*

According to the PBS series "American Experience," "it was a flu unlike any other. People could be healthy in the morning, and dead by nightfall. Others died more slowly, suffocating from the buildup of liquid in their lungs." Mislabeled Spanish Influenza, it was really a pandemic. 675,000 Americans died, more than 25% of the population was sick. The first wave hit in the spring of 1918. The second wave came in the fall, "October saw the epidemic's full horror: more than 195,000 people died...there was a national shortage of caskets." Philadelphia advertised in Elmira for embalmers.

On September 20th, the Elmira *Star-Gazette* headline read, "influenza and whooping cough threaten invasion of Elmira." The disease seems to have been carried by soldiers and brought home as a "killer virus" as they returned from Europe. On September 27th, the *Star-Gazette* reported that, "all draft troop movements deferred until epidemic is checked." Elmira papers reported the deaths of five Elmira servicemen from influenza between September 30 and October 8.

The City of Elmira Health Officer, Dr. R. B. Howland, warned against over-eating. "People who are inclined to eat heartily are prone to colds and a cold may bring on influenza." He also recommended more stringent measures in case of whooping cough, "the home must be placarded and the individual having the disease must wear a red band on the arm when outside the house the band to bear the words, "Whooping Cough."

On October 3rd, it was reported that the flu had come to Elmira College. MacKenzie Cottage was quarantined with patients being transferred to that building. None of the cases were considered serious although there was one case of pneumonia. The next day Dr. Howland declared that there were "not enough patients in Elmira to cause worry." Sadly, Elmirans learned of the suicide of Colonel Charles B. Hagedorn, a former Elmiran and Acting Commandant of Camp Grant in Illinois. Apparently his death was caused by the "stress imposed on him by the epidemic of Spanish Influenza and pneumonia which had caused 500 deaths at the camp."

Articles began to run in the Elmira papers with headlines, "Spanish Influenza, What It Is and How It Should Be Treated." The Elmira *Herald* reported about Vicks Vapo-Rub, describing its origin and application, noting that Vicks was "comparatively new to New York State" and that over six million jars were sold the previous year. Catarrhal Jelly was promoted, as was Horlick's Malted Milk—"the diet during and after influenza."

With World War I underway, Elmirans worried about the Liberty Loan Drive. The goal was $3,566,400. On October 10th, the *Star-Gazette* claimed that the, "Spanish influenza outbreak here is trivial compared to lack of interest taken by Elmirans in the Fourth Liberty Loan Subscription." Another issue for the citizenry to consider was whether or not the city should bond for $40,000 to build a municipal garbage plant.

On October 15th the *Herald* announced, "The lid is on. Elmira is closed to prevent further spread of Spanish Influenza." The night before a "Quarantine Order" had been declared by the Board of Health. The Order read, "all theaters, churches and Sunday schools, public, parochial schools and kindergartens, public libraries and art galleries, pool and billiard rooms and bowling alleys, all places where public meetings of every name and nature including meetings of fraternal, social and labor organizations are held public and private dances, all public funerals to be discontinued, all business houses and mercantile houses in the City of Elmira to discontinue any special sales of any article or articles, that various hospitals restrict visitors, that people overcrowding street cars and that all persons refrain from visiting homes or other places where there is sickness."

ELMIRA STAR-GAZETTE.

Of 1,671 Influenza Cases in Elmira Many Patients Now Are Recovering

Vast Amount of Illness Reported Between October 14 and 22, but Figures Show That Peak of Epidemic Here Has Been Reached—Other Cities, However, Have Experienced Increase in Disease, After First Lull Before Illness Is Wiped Out—One Hundred and Two Cases of Pneumonia Since October 14—Quarantine Will Continue Until Better Conditions Prevail.

Elmira Hospitals Are Filled; May Utilize Elks' Home Soon

Thirty-Two Deaths In Elmira Since Oct. 1 Due to Epidemic

Twenty-nine Citizens Have Died From Influenza and Three From Pneumonia— Local Mortality Rate Low Compared to Other Cities.

Both headlines in the *Star-Gazette* (Elmira, New York) October 23, 1918 page 2.

Street cars were to be fumigated and disinfected every 24 hours. "Coughing and sneezing in public places" were to be considered a "misdemeanor in the future" and would be "punishable by law." The same was true for " the practice of visiting homes where there is illness." Vice President F. H. Hall of the E.W. L. & R. R. Co. offered the use of the Roricks dance pavilion as a hospital for cases if necessary. The Hotel Gotham, working with the Red Cross, set aside 36 rooms to be used for an emergency hospital.

The economic impact of the epidemic was significant. The street car company reported a $10,000 loss. On October 18th American LaFrance had 110 men off 45 of them sick, Kennedy Valve had 126 off with 54 sick. Coal mining production dropped 50%. The Chemung County Fuel Administrator said, "Elmirans may have to cut down the number of rooms heated in their homes." The *Herald* reported that, "Seven merry maidens who sing tra-la and dance la la and merrily laugh ha ha are wishing Health Officer Howland hangnails for the rest of his days...." They were the girls of the "Who's Who" musical comedy running at the Majestic Theater when the Quarantine was imposed. While the children may have enjoyed no school, Halloween suffered as a result of influenza.

On Friday, November 1st, the quarantine was lifted except for funerals, dances and Sunday schools. It was reported that since the Quarantine went into effect on October 15th, Elmira was visited by 2,740 influenza cases causing 68 deaths and 155 pneumonia cases resulting in 20 deaths.

Twenty-one Elmira churches refused to accept permission to open churches on Sunday until the ban was lifted entirely—they wondered about the decision to open schools on Monday and keeping Sunday schools closed. The Liberty Loan Subscription would go over the top by $342,400 and the plan for a municipal garbage plant was rejected by the voters.

Elmira turned to celebrating the armistice and the joy of returning soldiers, but influenza lingered. On December 13, 1918 the *Star-Gazette* reported that the "Board of Health realizing that Elmira is not free of prevalent disease orders that all homes having influenza patients be quarantined two weeks."

First Day of School -
The Norton Sisters' Kindergarten

by Diane Janowski

The concept of an "infant school" as a separate learning environment for pre-school children goes back to 1779 in Strasbourg, Austria. The idea was refined, and by 1820 there were several infant schools in Europe. German scholars experimented and renamed the concept "Kindergarten" which is German for "children's garden" in 1840. Women were trained under this model and opened kindergartens throughout Europe. The first kindergarten in the United States opened in Watertown, Wisconsin in 1856.

Young educator Miss Mary Emily Norton taught at Elmira's Diven School around 1880. She was a forward thinker and knew what was happening in the German education system.

Mary Emily quit her position at Diven School and went to New York City to study this "kindergarten" idea and how she could implement it in Elmira.

She came back to Elmira in September 1885 armed with ideas of blocks, paints and crayons, scissors and paper, and the knowledge that she learned while in New York City.

She figured out which local parents had children of the right age and sent them letters that read, "Miss Mary Emily Norton begs to announce that her Kindergarten School will open Jan. 4, 1886 at the residence of Mr. H. S. Redfield, corner of Park Place and Fifth St." The Norton Kindergarten took students as far as the second grade if parents desired.

Twenty mothers quickly signed up their children. On the first day of school there were three teachers – Miss Mary Emily, her sister Miss Frances Norton, and Fräulein Theodor.

The curriculum included music, reading, writing, art, and lessons in the German language by Fräulein Theodor. Outdoor excursions were frequent to Grove Park and Rorick's Glen to study nature.

DISAPPEARING from the Elmira scene is this house at 266 W. Second St., where for more than 40 years the Misses Emily and Frances Norton conducted their famous children's school. For many years it was the city's only kindergarten. The school was abandoned in the 1920s. The building is coming down to clear a site for business expansion.

Image from the Elmira *Advertiser*, July 3, 1953.

And, of course, children with birthdays were a wonderful excuse to eat ice cream and cake. According to the June 27, 1939 *Star-Gazette*, "Misses Nortons' pupils had fun while they learned amicable group cooperation with a minimum of disciplinary coercion." The Norton philosophy was "Let the children express themselves as they will. Children are individuals and should not be regimented."

In 1889, the school moved to its permanent location of 226 West Second Street (now in the parking lot of today's Weis Market). Miss Mary Emily kept a diary of the happenings at her school. She recorded the names of new students including some as young as three-years old. She had several mute students, and eventually had a Chinese student named Hugh King Lee who started at age 13. Hugh was privately tutored by Miss Mary Emily, and he went on to graduate from Yale University.

In 1894, Miss Frances Norton followed in her sister's footsteps, and enrolled at the Buffalo Kindergarten Training Center's two year program. She returned to Elmira in 1896 and took over the kindergarten activities, while Miss Mary Emily concentrated on the first grade. In 1907, Miss Frances was persuaded by Mrs. J. Sloat Fassett to start a kindergarten program for Elmira's city school system. She stayed for nine years, but then returned to her sister's school. Faculty at the Norton school varied from year to year, and included Miss Eleanor Magee, Miss Mildred Ellis, Miss Ruth Hardy, Miss Wood, Miss Ernestine French, Fritz Duhl, and Professor John Bostleman.

Miss Mary Emily died in 1924, and Miss Frances continued until ill health forced her to quit in 1929. The house reverted to being a residence for the Nortons' niece Mary Price.

More than 500 Elmira scholars graduated from this little school.

ANCHORAGE DOING GOOD WORK; ANNUAL RECEPTION NEXT WEEK

Management Asks Friends to Aid by Presence and Offerings—Need of Financial Assistance is Great Now—Established Sixteen Years Ago —Three Additions to the Building Since That Time—Those Who Are in Charge

From the Elmira *Gazette and Free Press*, June 15, 1906 page 6.

The Anchorage

by James Hare

"The worst holocaust in Elmira's history occurred last night when three lives were snuffed out in a terrible fire at the Anchorage, 955 College Avenue. Three little babes were the victims and though their grief maddened mothers made frantic endeavors to reach their suffocating little ones, an impassable wall of flame barred the way and rendered all efforts unavailing." (Elmira *Daily Advertiser* on March 9, 1903).

The Anchorage opened with Helen L. Bullock as its founder and president. According to the "Annual Report of the Anchorage,"(1900) "The prison work of the Elmira Council W.C.T.U. revealed the great need for a police matron to care for the women and girls who are brought to our police station.... So many of these thoughtless, wayward girls needed training in an industrial Christian home in order to save them that we found it necessary to organize the Anchorage, which was done April 1, 1890."

In the last half of the 19th century Elmira's growth led to her renown as "the Queen City of the Southern Tier." With a population of over 30,000, by the end of the century she had earned a national and regional reputation as both an economic and cultural center. According to Joan Jacobs Brumberg, in her article on "Ruined Girls...." "it was the kind of city to which young women might be drawn for entertainment; for work in burgeoning industries, hotels and stores; for the opportunity to meet young railroad men; for education at the high school, commercial or collegiate levels; or for anonymity when they found themselves in trouble."

Following the Civil War, the Temperance Movement had a significant influence on Elmira. White, middle-class church women were brought into close contact with Elmira's disenfranchised population: namely the laboring classes comprised of recent immigrants and African Americans. Urged on by Protestant women with a mission, the Orphan's Home (1868), the Home for the Aged (1874), and the Industrial School

(1878) were incorporated, along with the development of the Elmira Reformatory (1876) led by Zebulon Brockway. In 1885, the first Chemung
County chapter of the Women's Christian Temperance Union was established in Elmira, with Helen L. Bullock as president. The W.C.T.U. also
"approached women of the various church missionary societies to form the
Elmira Women's Council for the Uplift of Women."

        The Anchorage was opened "in the heart of a residential neighbor-
hood" for girls who had "fallen or who were in circumstances that might
lead to their fall from want of employment, from destitution or from evil
associates." According to Elisabeth Carr Chapman's article in the *Chemung
County Historical Journal,* "the first site of the Anchorage was a house at the
corner of Roe Avenue and Davis Street. When it was sold, the organization was able to buy a large house at 955 College Avenue for $4,250 cash.
Of this amount, $2,500 was borrowed and the balance raised from gifts,
including one in the final hour from a critically ill W.C.T.U. member whom
"the Lord directed to give a bank note of $611. The lady recovered and later
became a trustee, Mrs. Harriet Brown."

        The school had 53 rooms with each of the forty or so girls hav-
ing their own room. There was a laundry and sewing room with donations
accepted of food, clothing, bedding, desks and chairs. The girls generally
ranged in age from twelve to eighteen years of age. Chapman described their
routines, "rising at 5:30; breakfast at 6:30 followed by prayers; morning du-
ties in the laundry or kitchen; noon dinner; 2 p.m. school; 4 p.m. recreation;
5:30 supper; 7 to 8 study; 8:30 worship; 9 to bed. Saturday morning was
bath time; Sunday was church with a chaperone. Besides housework, they
were given instruction in elementary English, botany, music, some Latin
and French, physical culture, gardening."

        There was an award system for behavior, with demerits for "mis-
takes." Girls were addressed by first name only. No talking was allowed in
rooms or halls. Punishment for undesirable behavior might be sitting at a
"disgrace" table and no dessert. Good behavior could lead to "four desserts
a week plus privileges like concerts and picnics and ice cream on Sunday
nights."

Acceptance for care at the Anchorage was a product of the W.C.T.U. network providing a statewide referral service as well as the needs locally. The "ledger" had a vocabulary which helped describe situations. A "ruined" girl was an unwed mother, a "betrayed" girl had been promised marriage in exchange for sex and "claimed" was used when referring to sexual assault. An entry for July 12, 1905 explains that "Irene was brought by her mother who is a poor widow supporting herself and three children by going out to work. Irene is fifteen-years-old and not as bright as ordinary girls of that age. Being left alone so much her mother feared she would be led astray or get into trouble by dissolute companions...." On February 14, 1900 Jenny "was brought here by her father who is a farmer near Erin. She expects to become a mother about the last of April... Father brings farm products in payment of board." Gertrude was born May 4, 1900, and on August 31st Jenny and the child went to do house work.

As the twentieth century got underway, domestic service as a source of employment began to decline and wider options became available. The Anchorage dropped its services to pregnant girls entirely in 1907. It became the Helen L. Bullock Industrial (Training) School and changed its mandate to vocational training for young women aged twelve to sixteen-years-old.

The institution would close in 1920. Mrs. Bullock said the reason was increased expense and the difficulty of securing efficient teachers. The Fire Marshall attributed it to lack of safety in the building. Also the Salvation Army had opened a house nearby which depleted the number of girls attending. The building became a multiunit apartment house and was destroyed by fire in December of 2010 and demolished in March of 2011.

Old Time Aviation Excitement

By Diane Janowski

We all love air shows. Lincoln Beachey's "flying aeroplane" was the first airplane seen over Elmira according to the Elmira Telegram July 9, 1911. "Although Elmira is but little removed from Hammondsport, New York [Glenn Curtiss built and tested his airplanes there)] and the field of much flying experiments, there are but few people here who have actually seen an aeroplane in flight.".... "[Beachey's] flights here will illustrate the rapid progress made in the new art of flying and will include all of the fancy frills of the most daring and accomplished birdmen." The flights took place at the Maple Avenue driving park. Beachey had already enjoyed his showmanship for building and piloting a dirigible at previous aviation meets. The Toledo, Ohio 1910 census lists him as an "aeronaut."

San Francisco native, Lincoln Beachey came to be known as "The World's Greatest Aviator" earlier in 1911 when he filled in for an injured stunt pilot at the Los Angeles International Air Meet. He flew his plane up 3,000 feet when the engine failed. The plane nose-dived and Beachey wrangled the plane into control and safely landed. Apparently no pilot had ever survived a nose-dive before this time and he became an instant sensation. He also saw the reaction of the crowd to his death-defying plummet. He saw the value of headlines for bringing crowds to his exhibitions. He began doing things to create a lot of excitement.

Beachey joined Glenn Curtiss's aviation exhibition team and flew Curtiss planes with moveable aileron (those small flaps on the edges of wings).

In 1911 at the US-Canadian Carnival, he was the first pilot to fly over Niagara Falls – both the American and Canadian Falls. At one point, he dove down to about 20 feet over the river at the bottom of the falls.

He also held the first record for an aviator crossing from Canada to the US. Later in the same year he raced a train at a meet in Chicago, even touching the wheels of his plane on the moving train.

Beachey came back to Elmira in 1914 for another show. Elmira *Telegram* advertisment.

He invented "Figure 8s", the "Dutch Roll," the "Spiral Glide," the "Dip of Death," the "Corkscrew Flip-flop," and with the help of Glenn Curtiss's powerful stunt plane perfected the masterpiece of his aviation tricks - his famous "Inside Loop."

Beachey held the unofficial world's record for height when on July 31, 1912 over Bath, New York his plane rose to 6,200 feet, and in a second flight that day a height of 6,500 feet. He said he would try it again when he found an official "Aero Club observer" as a witness. His technique was full of danger and accidents happened. While practicing a somersault in Hammondsport in October 1913 with Curtiss's plane, Beachey struck a hangar. It collapsed instantly killing a female spectator and injuring several others on a roof. He retired from aviation for a short while, but he could not stay away.

Beachey designed himself a new plane for looping, as other pilots were now doing the same stunt. Everytime one of them set a record for looping, he quickly broke it.

Beachey's manager thought of a money making scheme with car racer Barney Oldfield. The idea was for Beachey in his plane to race Oldfield's car on the ground. They took turns "winning." The crowds loved their competitions.

Beachey and Oldfield toured the country including a 1914 stop in Elmira at the Maple Avenue Driving Park.

In 1915, he unveiled his Beachey-Eaton monoplane at the Pana-ma–Pacific International Exposition in San Francisco. He made a loop, but when he tried to pull the plane out of its inverted position, the wings broke and he crashed into San Francisco Bay. Apparently he survived the crash, but drowned while waiting for the rescue team. Many thousands of spectators saw the crash.

Everyone knew his name.

Sources:

http://www.nationalaviation.org/beachey-lincoln/
Elmira *Telegram*, July 9, 1911 "Beachey, Daring Birdman, To Visit Us."
Elmira *Telegram*, October 12, 1913
Elmira *Telegram*, May 24, 1914
Elmira *Telegram*, March 28, 1915
Buffalo *Courier*, June 22, 1911 page 1

The Elevation of the Railroad

by James Hare

Elmira No Longer in Halves as Railroad Takes to Stilts

Headline story on Elmira *Star-Gazette* October 24, 1934 page 1.

Thirteen days wasted. That was the reported result of a seven hour traffic survey completed on Water Street at the Erie crossing in April, 1926. During that period 18,776 people crossed the tracks (sometimes twice) while trains and light engines steamed by blocking traffic. While some waited up to five minutes, the estimate was based on one minute per person. That came to 18,776 minutes =311 hours = 13 days.

County Historian Tom Byrne wrote that "the elevation of the railroads in the early 1930's was an immense project, comparable to the long-discussed north-south arterial highway (Clemens Center Parkway) of the 1970's." The elevation project was first proposed in 1925. It took eight years to arrange the financing with the state, railroads and local funds. Leading proponents were John J. Mantell of Elmira and vice president of the Erie Railroad, and Frank Tripp, Elmira *Star-Gazette* publisher.

When President Millard Fillmore and Secretary of State Daniel Webster visited Elmira in 1851 to celebrate the completion of the Erie Railroad the tracks were west of the "little village". Elmira, at that time, was centered around Lake and Baldwin Streets although people had begun relocating westward. It would be the 1920's before Main Street became the primary shopping district. By 1925, it was clear the elevation was necessary.

The Erie project was estimated at $3.2 million and the Lackawanna cost was to be $303, 500 according to Bryne. Fifteen at grade Erie crossings and six Lackawanna crossings were eliminated. Originally the city was expected to pay 25% of the cost but that was eventually reduced to 1%.

Construction of the 1,700-foot Erie viaduct from the northerly side of Second Street to the northerly abutment of the river bridge began on December 1, 1933 "through the coldest winter the community has experienced in many years...ground temperatures far below zero...." Up to 500 men worked on the project. (47,000 cubic yards of concrete, 3,365,000 pounds of reinforced steel, 6,281,000 pounds of structured steel, 71,000 barrels of the cement, 400,000 cubic yards of earth)

United Elmira Day was to be October 25, 1934. Headlines read "Spirit of Mardi Gras To Mark Celebration of United Elmira." Special attractions in theaters were offered and Elmira merchants offered $300 in cash prizes. Customers who purchased any item of 50 cents or more would receive a ticket for the drawing. (there were 43 cash gifts, $100, $50, $25, five gifts of $10, ten $5 gifts and twenty five $1 gifts). Extra tickets could be purchased for $5.

Thousands gathered to hear Governor Lehman proclaim, "I now declare the crossing open" as he severed a rope across Water Street. The *Star-Gazette* pronounced it, "The Great Reunion", the end of the "old Chinese Wall" through the center of the city. City Manager Florence J. Sullivan said, "life and limb will no longer be subject to the hazard of grade crossings in the heart of the city. Real estate...will increase in value."

Miss Helen M. Schneider of 601 Robinson Street was given the $100 grand prize from the merchants. That was the good news. Sadly, the elimination of grade crossings meant the end of the line for Crossing Watchmen. For 85 years from dawn to dusk they had protected the public. In the evening red lanterns had been faithfully lighted by the Watchmen to flag trains in the dark should necessity warrant. Their jobs were lost to progress.

Did Sally ever find her family?

By Diane Janowski

I recently came across an "Information Wanted" advertisement in the Gettysburg (PA) *Compiler* dated August 11, 1819 – nearly 197 years ago. It was written by Sally Gearhart of Elmira, Tioga County. She was looking for her missing family that she had not seen in 28 years.

Her advertisement says that she was taken prisoner by the Indians during St. Clair's Defeat in the Northwest Territory along the western border of Ohio on November 4, 1791. After eleven months of "cruel treatment by the savages" she was "ransomed by a benevolent Frenchman of Detroit, who had been trading with the Indians."

Her request for information did not say how she came to be in Ohio or whether she ever reunited with her family. That made me curious. So what could I make from this.

The ad said she was born Sally Stone. Her father was James Stone (her mother was James' second wife) and they had lived in Bucks County, Pennsylvania, then moved to Little Whiteley Creek. I think she refers to Whiteley Creek near Masontown, Pennsylvania. Sally said her father died at this location, but I found that he actually died in Bucks County [in 1789]. Her mother then married Peter Walded (maybe Walden), and moved to Post St. Vincent, on the Wabash River in Ohio, where he was "killed by the natives."

Sally's husband was James Fullen, whom she believed was also killed. Sally's mother then married Lewis Surveyor. Sally's sister Margaret married a man named Malbuff, and her other sister Betsey married a man named Smith. Sally had three brothers, James, Samuel and John. Also her half-brother Elias Stone married Betsey Baldwin at Forks of Cheat.

Ancestry.com says

Sally (Sarah) born October 3, 1772 in New York – died April 24, 1833 buried in Gearhart cemetery in Veteran.

Married James Fullen in 1788 in Bucks County
Married John H. Hoody (or Woody) in 1793 in Elmira
Married Tobias Gearhart (1788-?) in Elmira before 1810
Son Tobias Denyk Gearhart II in Elmira in 1810-1886
Son Aaron Denyk Gearhart Elmira 1813-1891

Sally is buried in the Gearhart Cemetery in Veteran Township on Lintal Drive off of Route 13.

INFORMATION WANTED.

At the time of general St. Clair's defeat 28 years ago, the subscriber was taken prisoner by the Indians, and thereby separated from her kindred, of whom she has not heard since. She was the daughter of James Stone, by his second wife—was born in Bucks county, Pennsylvania. Her father removed from thence to Little Whiteley Creek, about three miles from its confluence with the Monongahela river, where he died. At this place her half-brother, Elias Stone (who married Miss Betsey Baldwin) then lived, who had a sister living about forty miles above, at a place called the Forks of Cheat. At Little Whiteley Creek her mother was married to Peter Walded, who removed with his family to Post St. Vincent, on the Wabash river, where he was killed by the natives. Here she married James Fullen, (who she believes was killed) and her mother to Mr. Lewis Surveyor. One of her sisters (Margaret Stone) married a Mr. Malbuff—the other (Betsey) a Mr. Smith. She had three brothers, James, Samuel and John Stone. After eleven months cruel treatment by the savages, she was ransomed by a benevolent Frenchman of Detroit, who was then trading among the Indians.

SALLY GEARHART.
Elmira, Tioga co. N. Y. June, 1819.

Gettysburg *Compiler* (Gettysburg, Pennsylvania) August 11, 1819 page 3.

The First Steele Memorial Library

by James Hare

"When the new teacher entered Mexico Academy, the members of the faculty, as well as the students, were personally unknown to him, and he had studied with interest a catalogue containing their names. It chanced, however, that a change had been made after the catalogue was printed, and he was, therefore, entirely unprepared, when he met the music teacher, to see a dark-haired, brown-eyed young lady of vivacious, candid manner and an altogether indescribable charm." A lady, who was present at that first meeting observed, "it is impossible to give in words any idea of the look with which Professor Steele regarded Miss Baker. Between his evident admiration and his surprise his face was a study. I think it was a case of love at first sight...." in less than a year (July 1859) they were married in what Mrs. George Archibald, in her book on Joel Dorman Steele, described as a "marriage of true minds."

The Steeles came to Elmira in 1866, when Dr. Steele became the principal of Elmira Free Academy. Their home was at 352 W. Clinton Street and called, "The Gables." He became an author of textbooks and Esther Baker Steele became his, "advisor, secretary, research assistant, verifier of facts, reviser, critic and proof reader" as well as co-author and an author in her own right. According to the *Star-Gazette* of September 2, 1922, "Dr. Steele saw himself changed from the plain school master to the well nigh millionaire author. He enjoyed sixteen years of authorship with royalties continuing after his death."

Dr. Steele died in 1886 with a vision of a public library for Elmira unfulfilled. (It should be noted that when the present Park Church building opened in 1875, the room now used as the minister's study was a library open to the public. It remained the only public library until the opening of the first Steele Memorial Library, according to Park Church records.) Esther Baker Steele made his vision a reality. According to Eva Taylor in the *Chemung County Historical Journal*, "the first formal step was to found the Steele Memorial Library Association." Mrs. Steele was elected the first

President of the Board
of Trustees when they
met at her home on
July 20, 1894.

Years earlier,
on August 11, 1892,
land had been pur-
chased by the Elmira
YMCA for the pur-
pose of erecting a
building for the youth
of Elmira. It was to be
designed by the archi-
tectural firm of Pierce
and Bickford and
would be located at
the corner of Lake and
Market Streets (site
of the Five Star Bank).
The Y decided they did

First Steele Memorial Library, uncredited postcard.
Courtesy of the Barnes Library.

not need all the land, and on August 27, 1894 an agreement was reached
with the recently incorporated Steele Memorial Library Association giving them the corner lot. Mrs. Steele agreed with the trustees of the YMCA
"to build a five story building—the fourth and fifth floor to house the library" with the lower floors and basement to rent to supplement the funds
of the library. In fact, four buildings under one roof would be built, each
separated by a fire wall, but when in use open through the hallways.

The cornerstone of the library was laid May 27, 1895, and the
building would be opened to the public in August 1899. According to the
Star-Gazette of September 2, 1922 the total cost was $65,000 ($1,857,050
in 2015 dollars) with the "building itself costing over $40,000." Mrs. Steele
agreed to turn the building over to the Library Association and to "place
on the shelves of the library books of value not less than $25,000." On Au-
gust 2, 1899, the *Star-Gazette* reported, "at the present time there are about
4,000 volumes in the reference library and 2,000 in the circulating library

and the building itself is one that is not excelled for beauty and convenience for its size in the state." On the same day the Elmira *Daily Advertiser* observed, "what joy shone upon the faces of many of the visitors yesterday as they saw in the tier after tier of valuable books visions of feasts during the coming months after a long time of hungering for certain coveted books."

Mrs. Steele was anxious for her niece, Mrs. Kate Deane Andrew, to become the head librarian at the new library. Unfortunately she did not meet the state qualifications. Not to be deterred, Mrs. Steele reached out to her friend Chancellor James Roscoe Day of the University of Syracuse. (Dr. Steele had left a bequest of $50,000 to the University to found a chair of Theistic Science, Mrs. Steele facilitated the funding by relinquishing her own annuities, and aided projects for additional buildings and was bestowed with a degree of Doctor of Literature in 1892, she became a trustee in 1895). Soon thereafter, the Syracuse University Library School was established. Her niece was enrolled in September 1896, and two years later became the first graduate. She became the first librarian at the Steele Memorial Library serving for forty years in that position.

Esther Baker Steele passed away at her home on the morning of November 23, 1911. In her obituary she was described as "a teacher herself, in the truest and noblest acceptation of the term, her heart, soul, and mind were always in constant and helpful sympathy with every effort to advance education." Chancellor Day of Syracuse University officiated at the funeral.

At the time of Mrs. Steele's death, the library had 18,776 volumes with 10,483 borrowers. Total circulation was 72,850 volumes, 53,703 to adults and 19,147 to juveniles according to the Annual Report for June 30, 1911 to June 30, 1912.

Some Early Hotels in Elmira

by Diane Janowski

The Rathbun Hotel was at the corner of East Water and Baldwin Streets, now the site of the Chemung Canal Trust Company. Rotograph Co. postcard courtesy of the Barnes Library.

The very first "publick house" in Elmira was a straggly log cabin on East Water Street just east of Sullivan Street. It was run by a man named Granger.

The second was Seely's Tavern run by the widow Seely on the corner of East Water and Conongue Street (now Madison Avenue). It was there that the Duc d'Orleans, later King Louis Philippe of France and his two brothers stayed there for 10 days in 1797. After their stay in old New-town, they acquired a Durham boat and sailed down the Chemung and Susquehanna rivers to Wilkes-Barre, Pennsylvania. Seely's Tavern became the Kline House. Mr. Kline also ran the ferry across the Chemung River from the same location.

Next came the Black Horse Tavern on the corner of East Water and Lake Streets. Including its horse barn, it took up nearly a whole block. It was razed in 1848.

It was at Teall's Tavern, in the vicinity of Sullivan Street, that Elmira probably got its name. Frequent guest Judge Amanuel Coryell of Owego was quite smitten with the tavern owner's little daughter Elmira, and suggested that her beauty matched the town's beauty. He asked the Board of Trustees to change the name of Newtown to Elmira. History books describe Teall's Tavern as "a comfortable room, large, filled with easy chairs, warm and cosy in winter and bright and airy in summer, and it had an odor that seemed to have become soaked into the floor, the furniture, the walls, and the ceiling: a compound smell that was not precisely disagreeable, borrowed from old buffalo robes, horses, a pinch of tobacco smoke, and the fumes of rare old whiskey."

On the southside of East Water Street between Lake and Baldwin Streets was the first Mansion House run by Judge Bundy. A second Mansion House was built in 1830 on Lake Street where the Mohawk market eventually stood. The Mansion House burned down in 1849 and Silas Haight rebuilt it as Haight's Hotel on the same spot. It also burned down and was rebuilt as the Hathaway House.

The construction of the Chemung Canal brought a large number of laborers to Elmira. One favorite location for them was Hogan's Tavern on the site of today's Chemung Canal bank on East Water Street. When the canal was finished in 1833, downtown Elmira breathed a sigh of relief for these laborers' wild antics agitated the neighbors.

On this same site was built a three-story hotel that was eventually called the Brainard Hotel. It burned in 1849 and was rebuilt. Owner E.R. Brainard died within a year. His widow sold it to John T. Rathbun who called it the Rathbun Hotel.

Many famous people have visited Elmira, but the city entertained probably its greatest group of celebrities on night in 1851, when President Millard Fillmore and his Secretary of State, Daniel Webster stayed at the

Mansion House, and Stephen A. Douglas and William H. Seward, later on Lincoln's cabinet,, stayed at the Rathbun Hotel. History books claim Fillmore spoke from the Mansion Hose and Douglas from the Rathbun's balcony.

One of the most frequent visitors of the Rathbun Hotel was Mark Twain (our Samuel Clemens). Mark spent many hours playing billiards in the Mayfair Room.

Elmira's 1868 directory lists 64 hotels. The list includes the Patterson House at Baldwin and Market, the Temperance House, and the American Hotel (also known as the Frasier House), and the St. James Hotel. The Chemung House was opposite the Patterson House.

The Red Jacket Inn on the south side of Carroll Street between Lake and Baldwin was frequently vistited by Rev. Thomas K. Beecher. The Pennsylvania House on West Water Street later became the Wyckoff House. The Alice Frances Hotel stood where Weis Market is today. The Arlington House was down in Bulkhead, and the Delevan Hotel was at West Clinton and Railroad Avenue.

Rural visitors preferred the West End Hotel on the north side of West Water Street, the Homestead Hotel, the Buckbee Hotel on East Water Street, and Sickle's Hotel at Lake and Standish Streets.

Elmira's largest hotel was the Mark Twain Hotel that opened in 1929 right before the stock market crash. A six-story addition opened in 1939.

The Langwell Hotel opened in 1896 with 54 rooms.

The Ku Klux Klan makes an Impression on Elmira

by James Hare

Distribute Klan Literature
Throughout City of Elmira;
Its Purposes Are Outlined

Booklets Left at Homes,
Stores and Other Places,
Said to Be "Missionary
Work" on Part of Ku
Klux Klan—Distributed
at Night.

Elmira *Star-Gazette* headline May 11, 1923 page 23.

Elmirans awoke on Friday morning May 11, 1923 to find a booklet left during the night at homes, stores and other places. The booklets were regarded as "missionary work" of the Ku Klux Klan according to the *Star-Gazette*. The "booklets are about eight by three inches in size with black cover and white lettering. *The Klu Klux Klan, Yesterday, Today and Forever* by William Joseph Simmons, Imperial Wizard." On St. Patrick's Day in 1923, the City of Binghamton had a similar experience. Broome County Historian Gerald Smith noted that the distribution of the literature in the middle of the night served as an announcement "that the KKK was coming." Major Earnest Smith, King Kleagle of the New York State Ku Klux Klan, was headquartered in Binghamton.

On June 28, 1923, the *Star-Gazette* reported that, "a decided stand against the Ku Klux Klan and its activities was taken by the local members of the Socialist party at the regular weekly meeting." Its resolution stated in part that, "The Klan has now reached New York State and its busy agents are eagerly initiating novices for a respectable consideration." A little over a year later, in October 1924, at the conclusion of the six week Billy Sunday Crusade in Elmira, the Klan left on the stage a basket of white chrysanthemums. Mr. Sunday stated that he welcomed the friendship of any organization that stood for Christ.

Lawrence Gooley wrote in the New York History Blog (June 11, 1914) that, "the original KKK died out in the 1870's after focusing on racial issues in the post Civil War period... but the KKK of the 1900's was a different animal...instead of just attacking Blacks, they added other targets: Jews, Catholics and immigrants ... Klansmen offered themselves as the defenders of 'Americanism—zealous patriots, religious fundamentalists and Caucasians."

The Klan got busy organizing in Elmira. The "alleged" Kleagle of the Elmira branch appeared in person at the *Star-Gazette* on August 12th, 1923 showing his certificate of authority, but not revealing his name to announce a meeting at Miller's Hall on South Main Street (the Miller block is 228-230 South Main). He stated that a "national lecturer of the order of the KKK would be present at the meeting to explain the principles and aims of the organization." The Kleagle was later identified as Richard Hendrikson of 264 West Henry Street.

The lecturer was the Rev. Nicholas U. Cossaboon of Buffalo, New York, who spoke to a packed hall of 600 people with an equal number turned away. The newspaper reported that "three young girls, two boys and two adults were the first to arrive... a young woman of about 16 years distributed Klan literature... five members of the police force were on hand." Among the questions Cassaboon answered were: Why is the Klan a secret organization?—his answer "Well are not the Knights of Columbus, Jewish societies and the Masonic orders secret?" Why do Klansmen wear hoods?—his answer "Well, what difference does it make whether a man is hooded—or hoodwinked?"

The night following the meeting the residents of Wellsburg, New York were startled about 9:30pm "when a mammoth cross was burned on Reservoir Hill near the village. A number of "hooded men were present," according the newspaper reports.

On July 24, 1924, it was reported that many Elmirans received invitations for a meeting at Elmira's Grotto Park on Wednesday evening July 30th. But the Chairman of the Grotto Committee objected, saying it had been rented without his knowledge under the name of the "Roosevelt Club" (the same subterfuge had been used at the Miller's Hall event the year before). Denied use of the Grotto Park, the "county meeting" was moved to Ithaca Street in Horseheads. It was attended by 1,500 persons and lasted from 7 to 11 o'clock in the evening. The *Star-Gazette* reported that "hundreds of automobiles were parked near the meeting place and Klansmen acted as traffic officers. No crosses were burned."

Rachel Dworkin, archivist at the Chemung County Historical Museum has written that, "in July 1925, Elmira was host to a Klorero, or annual gathering of New York State Klansmen, which lasted for days. The event included tours of the area historic sites, lectures, many bands and drill competitions, a parade down Church Street and a cross burning at the Fairgrounds. Over 6,000 people attended and numerous local businesses and organizations, including the Elmira Association of Commerce, took out ads in the event program." A *Star-Gazette* reporter attempted to enter the Fairgrounds but was told, "there is nothing for publication. The only way in which one may become acquainted with our activities is by being a member." The reporter could not hear the whispered password used by others.

A parade was scheduled for July 4th. It had been approved by city officials in February. The route was to begin at the lower end of Church Street, going west to Walnut Street, then south to Water Street, east to Lake Street, and then north to Church Street.

Early reports of 50,000 to 60,000 Klansmen marching proved to be exaggerated. The Klan parade was scheduled for 3pm with a Defense Day parade to follow at 7pm. All members of the Elmira police force were on duty. The Klan parade attracted, "several thousand visitors" to the city. Fifteen counties were represented. Participants were brought by trolley from the Fairgrounds to City Hall where they lined up. Part of the parade was drenched by a "downpour of rain." The marchers wore their white hoods and robes but without masks. Throughout the march, songs of religious and whimsical nature were "lustily sung" by the delegates. Many floats and bands participated. There were several scuffles along the route and police "effectively curbed" two anti Klan demonstrations.

The *Star-Gazette*, in a reflective article August 25, 1964), reported that, "suddenly it was over. The streets lost their long white lines of marchers and trundling floats. Street cars took the marchers away and the police didn't try to silence their sighs of relief that the parade had brought no real trouble."

On August 8, 1925 a much bigger parade would take place in the nation's capital, with a public meeting at the foot of the Washington Monument where the Klan could renew its vows. Three days prior, the Knights and women of the KKK of Chemung County left for Washington DC. Their "famous" Klan band traveled with them. It was anticipated that they would be one of the biggest delegations in the parade.

According to David M. Chalmers, in his book *Hooded Americanism*, "Many Klansmen had come prepared for the outing like the Elmira, New York contingent which set up its headquarters tent at the "one-hundred-percent-American camp..." Indeed, in the parade, the New Yorkers were, "led by the red-caped and hooded knights of Chemung County."

Author's note: Lawrence Gooley, in his blog, also noted that the Klan "wasn't for men only. There were several female branches of the KKK. Some wielded power by voting as a bloc and organizing boycotts against businesses owned by those considered less than 100% American."

The California Arrow
Visits Elmira

By Diane Janowski

Thomas Baldwin's "California Arrow" airship in
1904. Courtesy of the Smithsonian Institute.

In 1906, the Elmira *Sunday Telegram* advertised "Chemung County Fair September 17 - Two Daily Airship Flights by Captain Thomas S. Baldwin who demonstrated his ability to Navigate the Air at the St. Louis and Portland Expositions."

Baldwin was a showman and entrepreneur who specialized in balloon ascents, and in 1885 was the first person (or one of the first) to use a parachute at airshows. When he realized that the public was becoming bored with hot air balloons, he thought of a way to energize them.

Alberto Santos-Dumont in France had developed a dirigible – a balloon with a motor capable to maneuver through the air. Baldwin went to France to study Santos-Dumont's designs.

Baldwin was very interested in Hammondsport native Glenn Curtiss' motorcycle engines and the possibility of combining a balloon with an engine. In 1904, after seeing a Curtiss motorcycle in action, he ordered a V-Twin engine from the G. H. Curtiss Manufacturing Company, and mounted it on the California Arrow. A wooden cedar frame held the engine. The pilot stood on the frame, and used his weight to balance the airship.

The aerodynamic cigar-shaped gasbag was made of silk sealed with linseed oil, and filled with hydrogen. The bag was 54-feet long, and was painted silver. The whole apparatus including the engine weighed 520 pounds.

It was a triumph. Baldwin came to Hammondsport to meet Curtiss. The *California Arrow* was the first successfully flown dirigible in the United States.

The *Arrow* was scheduled for its first Elmira flight from the Chemung County Fair on the afternoon of Thursday September 19, 1906, but the rudder broke in practice. At about 6:30PM, the crew finished repairs and Baldwin took off for a trial flight around the fairgrounds. He promised to visit Elmira the next day.

The next morning, with winds slightly too strong for flying dirigibles, Baldwin ascended 2,000 feet above the fairgrounds, then headed south along the hills east of the city until he was over East Clinton Street. Then he turned right and cut across Elmira towards City Hall. When he was discovered, the fire bell tolled, factory whistles were blown, and Elmirans climbed to the tops of downtown buildings and expressed their shouts of approval. The *Arrow* circled City Hall, then turned north to fly over the north side for the return trip, much to the delight of Northsiders.

The airship landed at the fairgrounds after being airborne for thirty minutes. Baldwin stated that it was one of his most successful ascensions, and the first flight that he had made in New York State. It was also Elmira's first look at a dirigible.

The *California Arrow* was destroyed in the San Francisco earthquake on April 18, 1906. It, and four other airships were in storage at Baldwin's Market Street factory. With only one airship remaining, Baldwin moved to Hammondsport to be closer to Curtiss' expertise. In collaboration with Curtiss, Baldwin received an Army contract in 1908 and built three dirigibles. He built several airplanes between 1911 and 1913. In 1914, he built a dirigible for the Navy. Years later he enlisted in World War 1 in the Signal Corps as Chief of Balloon Inspection and Production. Baldwin died in Buffalo in 1923.

Sources:
Elmira *Gazette* September 12, 19 and 20, 1906
Elmira *Telegram* September 19 and 20, 1906
http://www.glennhcurtissmuseum.org/
http://welweb.org/ThenandNow/California%20Arrow.html
http://www.nationalaviation.org/baldwin-thomas/

The Mozart Theater

By James Hare

Postcard view of the Mozart Theater, circa 1910. Publisher unknown.

Professor Harold Hill, in the "Music Man," beguiled the residents of River City when he told them of "the electric thrill I once enjoyed when Gilmore, Pat Conway, The Great Creatore, W. C. Handy and John Philip Sousa all came to town on the very same historic day." For Elmirans, it was enough to just have John Philip Sousa. The Elmira *Advertiser* announced that "Famous Band Leader and His Company of Sixty Will Give Patriotic Concert—Mayor Harry N. Hoffman Will Introduce Mr. Sousa," on the evening of August 12, 1918.

This was Sousa's 26th annual concert tour. He was over sixty years old and had been commissioned as a lieutenant in charge of the musical forces training at the Great Lakes (Illinois) Naval Training Station. He had been ordered to France by the War Department, and he said he "hoped to have the pleasure of leading his musicians down the streets of Berlin to the tune of "Stars and Stripes" ahead of the courageous young men composing the American Army."

Two thousand people packed the theater to see the "March King." Every seat was taken, hundreds stood or were accommodated in the wings of the stage and in seats at the rear of the platform, despite it being the "hottest day of the season." Mayor Hoffman introduced Sousa who said that the appearance of the crowd indicated Elmirans, like the rest of the people of the world, were hungry for music. "There is a solace in it, that can be found in nothing else."

The three hour concert included vocal soloists, a coronet solo, and many encores. The Elmira *Telegram* observed that it featured "the best Yankee music... and not one note of German music." The *Advertiser*, reported that, "the Stars and Stripes was played as it had never been played in the city before...."

Sousa appeared at the Mozart ten years after its grand opening on November 23, 1908. Two days before the opening the *Star-Gazette* teased that, "when the first nighters enter the new Mozart Theater, Monday evening... they will see one of the most beautifully decorated and finest appointed playhouses of which any city outside New York can boast." The layout appeared "quite metropolitan." Patrons will be admitted by a door keeper and seated by ushers in tuxedo dress. The theater would have a marble lobby and a "gorgeous" proscenium arch. It could seat 1,398 with an orchestra, balcony and gallery. According to the *Star-Gazette*, "the provisions for the comfort of the patrons are admirable. On the first floor are retiring rooms, at the left for women and at the right for men." Dressing rooms and the boiler were in a separate building to insure safety. County Historian Tom Byrne noted that "seats for Mozart shows cost 50 cents for the first seven rows; 30 cents for the first three rows of the balcony; 10 cents for the gallery. House Rule No. 1 was Ladies are requested to remove their hats."

The Mozart Theater was located on East Market Street east of Baldwin Street. It was part of a chain of theaters and was the "first theater to be built in America by the united efforts of actors and managers." The actors group, the White Rats, gave money to Ed Mozart to build the theater. On opening night, John M. Connelly, President of the Chamber of Commerce said, "The year 1908... the beginning of a new era in Elmira history. The dream of a Bigger, Better, and Busier city is fast being realized."

Excitement for opening night was stimulated the day before when the featured act, "The Big Powers Hippodrome Elephants," arrived. They marched through the streets like a circus coming to town. The *Star-Gazette* reported that "crowds joined the march and by the time the elephants had reached their destination there were enough people in the procession to warrant a show being put on right there." The paper also claimed that a report which circulated that one of the elephants had lost his check and couldn't get his trunk was untrue.

The theater was jammed with 1700 people, 300 of them standing and 500 unable to get in. It was reported that "crowds thronged the streets seeking admission." The show opened with contortionists, followed by Major Doyle, the "diminutive Irish comedian," sketches, then Frances Gerard who pleased the community with "high class songs." The comedy feature of Slater, Perrin and Crosby was a "scream." The finale was the "Powers Hippodrome Elephants" which caused the audience to "sit in amazement at the marvelous feats of the wonderful beasts."

The Mozart eventually became the Strand turning mostly to movies. The last big night was May 16, 1959, when every seat was filled for an Elmira Civic Chorus spring concert. The building was razed in 1967.

Tremors, Quakes, and Rumbles in Chemung County

By Diane Janowski

New York State's first recorded earthquake occurred on December 18, 1737, with an epicenter near New York City. Sixteen other historic quakes were mentioned between 1638 and 2011.

Since 1925, Chemung County has felt six distinct rumbles. The first happened on February 27, 1925. A magnitude 6.2 earthquake centered in Quebec, shook the eastern part of the United States from New England to Mississippi at 9:23PM. The Elmira *Telegram* reported:

> *"Elmira felt the tremor about 9:25 o'clock. It caused pictures to dance on walls and floor lamps to shake in many homes. Chickens were knocked from their roosts at the Ralph Miller farm on lower*

ATTICA CENTER OF QUAKE FELT HERE ON MONDAY

From the Dunkirk *Evening Observer*, August 13, 1929.

Maple Avenue, while the glass was broken in the windows of the coop. Chandeliers in the farm residence were set swinging while cupboard doors were jarred open by the tremor.

At the home of Roy McEwen of 522 West First Street, the family noted a movement of pictures on the wall, while as Mr. McEwan said, "the floor lamp did a shimmy."

Julian Close reported that at his grocery store at 1059 Walnut Street the tremor was distinctly felt, and that the vibration lasted one and one-half minutes. He stated that the banana stalks were seen to move and that goods rattled on the shelves in the store.

Members of the Horseheads' American Legion were reminded of the days "over there" when the rocking sensation started.

Marsden Gerity of 415 William Street stated he returned home to find his French clock had stopped at 9:23."

Perhaps the most unusual report received was from some of the residents of Bridgman Street who were playing cards when the tremor was felt. They declared that to their surprise the table moved half way across the room.

Newspaper accounts did not speculate as to the location of the epicenter, but did say that it was felt in New York City, Hartford, Chicago, Washington, Philadelphia, Cleveland, Boston, Detroit, Richmond, and Montreal. Its magnitude was not reported, but the "seismograph experts at Georgetown University in Washington, DC described the quake as 'very severe.'"

The second earthquake (intensity VIII on the Mercalli scale), centered near Attica, New York, happened on August 12, 1929 at 6:25AM. The Elmira *Advertiser* reported that this tremor was felt in five states and Canada, and was enough to cause skyscrapers in New York City to sway. The magnitude is not known as the seismograph at Canisius College in Buffalo was jarred out of order after recording the principal upheaval. The laboratory reported that the main shock lasted twelve seconds. The Elmira *Advertiser* also said:

"*An Elmira grocer in the northwestern section of the city found that the shock had jumbled the canned goods out of their usual order. Bottles of syrup and catsup leaned against each other, and the apple butter section was all set to leap into the depths of the soap chips.*"

One Waverly woman is feeding her dog choice morsels today in penitence for a misplaced chastisement. She jumped out of bed Monday morning and whipped her Bruno for running around the kitchen so briskly that the dishes rattled. Later she learned that Bruno's galloping was the result, not the cause of the dancing crockery."

The third rumble took place on November 1, 1935, but the local news only reported "chickens leaving their roosts." It was a 6.1 magnitude quake that was centered in Quebec. The fourth tremor took place on September 5, 1944 and reached 5.8 on the Richter scale. It was centered between Massena, New York and Ontario, Canada. This one is listed as New York's largest earthquake to date. No damage was reported locally.

On October 7, 1983, the fifth rumble was a 5.3 quake centered in Blue Mountain Lake, New York. It gently shook Elmira and no damage was reported. My diary indicates at I felt it at 6:21AM. I remember waking up thinking I was having a bad dream because I was shaking. I remember hearing the pull chain on my ceiling lamp tinkling against the glass, and my dog, Dixie, rustling in the hall.

The sixth, and most recent, quake was a 5.8 magnitude centered near Washington DC on August 23, 2011 and many in our area felt that one.

Sources:

Elmira *Adveriser* August 12, 1929, November 2, 1935

Elmira *Star-Gazette*, September 6, 1944 and October 8, 1983

Elmira *Telegram*, February 28, 1925

Janowski, Diane, personal diary.

http://earthquake.usgs.gov/earthquakes/states/new_york/history.php

http://earthquake.usgs.gov/earthquakes/states/events/1983_10_07.php

The Orphan's Home

by James Hare

Katherine Westwood, in her *History of Elmira Child and Family Services 1864-1964*, records the sad story of a weeping mother leaving her baby at the Orphan's Home "because she had no money, and her father had turned her from his door. She returned two days later in haste and delight, her father had forgiven her, and she could bring the baby home. But alas, a kind lady, whose name the orphanage neglected to record had stopped by and seeing the baby, decided she would take it. There was nothing the poor mother could do...."

The Southern Tier Orphan's Home originated with the need for the relief of Civil War soldiers, their wives, widows and orphaned children during the last years of the war. A group of ladies from local Protestant Churches organized the Elmira Phoenix Hospital Aid Association incorporating on December 28, 1864 as the Ladies' Relief Association. In time the care and education of orphans and children needing temporary care outside the parental home became the principal objective.

In 1866, the old Holdridge house at the corner of Franklin and Fulton Streets on Elmira's south side was rented. The first children admitted were a ten-year old boy and his five-year old sister whose father had died in the Civil War. By the next year thirty children had been taken in.

The Southern Tier Orphan's Home was incorporated in 1868 with Mrs. David Decker as the first president of the board of managers. By 1874, it was decided to erect a building which would be located on the vacant lot next to what is today the Marion Center (located at the corner of Franklin and Fulton Sts). At the dedication in June of 1877, Mrs. Decker stated, "the purpose of the ladies from the first has been to conduct the Institution on the plan of a well regulated Christian family."

Over the years, funds were raised in a variety of ways: donations by Simeon Benjamin and David Decker, a one time appropriation by

The Orphans' Home on Franklin Street, circa 1855.
Photographer probably Elisha Van Aken.

the state legislature in 1871, and through annual donation days. According to the 1873 issue of the Southern Tier Orphan's Home News, "tubs of mackerel, tooth ache medicine... a large basket of beef, nine pair of shoes, three pair of drawers" were donated. In addition, there were lectures, concerts and strawberry festivals to raise funds. According to reports, "babies were brought from doorsteps or the river bank almost every day and none were turned away." They were brought by mothers and widower fathers, few questions were asked and none turned away." One matron exclaimed "cursed drink" sent many of them and "villainess fathers played their part."

The building was described as red brick "having wide halls, high ceilings, capacious well ventilated rooms with large windows." There were separate dormitories for boys and girls according to age. A small building at the back of the lot (the current home of the Elmira Garden Club) was the school house for grades one and two. It was equipped and serviced by School No. 3 (Parley Coburn) where children went to complete their grammar school education later going on to Elmira Free Academy.

The girls learned light housework and sewing while the boys sawed wood, brought up coal and "tidied" up the lot. Isabelle Ridall has written in the *Chemung Historical Journal* that, "the boys in a very unique manner do the scrubbing of the halls, using their feet for mop-sticks, and by shuffling back and forward steps perform a very neat and satisfactory piece of work." In 1925, Superintendent Mary E. Macomber reported, "On various occasions we were the guests of the managers of the Strand, Majestic, Lyceum and Regent Theaters. At Christmas time many friends sent in toys, candy, nuts etc. The "Big Sisters" of Elmira College attended to the well-filled stockings this is inevitable to a child's perfect Christmas. They also gave a Christmas party."

The Orphan's Home had such a successful baseball squad of five and ten-year-olds that the January 16, 1929 *Sunday Telegram* reported "these boys are practically in the same class with Gene Tunney and Man O' War as they have no opposition."

Unfortunately there were few if any records kept of the burials of children from the Orphan's Home. There are unmarked graves in the Fulton Street and Woodlawn Cemeteries for many of those who died while at the Home. The Orphan's Home was torn down in 1942 as the care for orphaned children evolved into the non for profit agency of Elmira Child and Family services, the forerunner of Family Services of Chemung County, Inc., which serves the public. The Orphanage movement generally disappeared with the growth of foster care and care management. Perhaps Katherine Westwood sums it up best, "It is easy to criticize these early days, but for the era the Home did a remarkable work...."

THE ORPHANS' HOME.

Annual Festival to Be Held in Bundy Hall This Week.

The annual Orphans' Home festival will be held this week in Bundy hall Wednesday, Thursday and Friday, November 18th, 19th and 20th. Dinner will be served each day from 12 until 2 o'clock. Supper from 5 until 7 o'clock.

The churches will serve in the following order:

Wednesday, November 18th: First Methodist, Hedding Methodist, First Baptist, Southside Baptist, Grace and Emmanuel.

Thursday, November 19th: First Presbyterian, North Presbyterian, Franklin Street Presbyterian, Trinity, Jewish Synagogue and Benton Street Baptist.

Friday, November 20th: Lake Street Presbyterian, Southport Corners' Presbyterian, St. Luke's Congregational, Park, Centenary Methodist, Riverside Methodist and German Evangelical.

The Orphans' Home is a worthy charity, and the coming festival should be liberally patronized. The society was incorporated as the Southern Tier Orphans' Home in 1868, and its substantial building in the Fifth ward is evidence of its prosperity and the good will it holds of the people. It is governed by a committee of ladies representing each of the churches of the city, from whom the officers are annually elected. More than 3,00 children have been cared for by the institution since it was established. It has no endowment or settled income—excepting $2,000, the gift of the late Simeon Rathbun, and of that only the interest can be used. It does not receive any money from the state. It depends for its support upon gifts from the charitable, the receipts from its annual festival and compensation made for care of dependent children by the supervisors.

Article in the *Star-Gazette* November 16, 1896 page 5.

Advertisement card for James E. Hardy. Zen Zeno supposed crossed Niagara Falls on Hardy's tightrope in 1897.

Zen Zeno "The River Kid"

by Diane Janowski

My job as City Historian requires me to answer questions – lots of questions. Many start with, "Did this really happen?" Sometimes I can answer, "Positively," or "Absolutely not." Then, there are the questions with answers that are somewhere in-between.

A few weeks ago, I received an email from a family that had a question about their father who lived in Elmira in the 1940s. "Dad" often spoke of his being four-years-old, walking out onto the winter ice on Brick Pond, falling through and drowning. Fortunately, he revived within a few minutes. The family wanted to know if the Elmira *Star-Gazette* reported the drowning incident. In the process of researching, I found out other things about the child that the family did not know. "Dad" was a frequent visitor of the St. Joseph's emergency room with at least two other incidents before the age of four – once for getting cut with a piece of glass, and the other for falling out of a cart - both newsworthy enough for the *Star-Gazette*. However, I did not find mention of his drowning. That is not to say that it did not happen. He may have recovered very quickly and not needed medical attention. The family did enjoy reading about the two other incidents.

Another recent question came from my childhood friend, Lu Randall, whose grandparents lived on my childhood street five houses up from my parents. Lu recalled her family's lore about the contractor who built that house at 506 Esty Street. She told me a long fun story. I asked myself if this could be true.

After much searching, I found a January 16, 1956 Kingston (New York) *Daily Freeman* article written by Frank Tripp about this contractor

(Zen Zeno, or rather, Oliver Hudson Hilton according to his birth certificate). Apparently, Frank and Zeno were old friends.

Tripp's article described Zeno as a high wire performer and contortionist, and the only (self-proclaimed) person to cross Niagara Falls on a tight rope without a balancing pole. Tripp said he had known Zeno for more than fifty years before knowing this tale.

Oliver Hilton was born in Niagara Falls in 1887. From an early age he was a daredevil and called himself "Zeno, the river kid." In the summer of 1896, exhibitionist tight roper James E. Hardy crossed Niagara Falls sixteen times on a rope with a balancing pole. After Hardy's crossings, laws were passed prohibiting tight roping across the river and the falls. The half-mile rope still stood in 1897 and ten-year-old Zeno claimed that the rope was calling him.

Young Zeno said he climbed onto the rope with no balancing pole and no shoes at 7 PM on September 16, 1897, on the Canadian side. Twenty minutes later, he was on the American side. Police quickly grabbed him and arrested him for illegal entry via a tightrope. When they found out he was a US citizen they let him go after a good hollering. As a historian, I find no proof supporting this story - as it was not part of a show, nor is there a police report on the matter. He was just a kid fooling around on a rope. But, did he really do what he said he did? I don't know.

Zeno, who had the "daredevil bug," claimed this tightrope walk changed the course of his life. He worked for circuses and vaudeville until 1917 when the US army claimed him and he became Oliver Hilton again. Oliver was 30 when he joined the Company H 310th Infantry in Elmira. His service papers did not give a reason, but he received an honorable discharge five months later.

Apparently, Oliver learned some new skills in the army. I found him in the "Situations Wanted" column of the *Star-Gazette* February 5,

1926 advertising himself as a carpenter with wallboard expertise. This must be how he came to build the Esty Street house at about the same time.

The 1920 census says he lived at 724 Robinson Street with his wife Maude (around the corner from Esty Street). He was listed as a contractor. The 1930 census lists him at 357 Riverside Avenue still with his wife, and his occupation was "furrier." The 1940 census says he lived at 402 Pennsylvania Avenue still with his wife, and he was still a furrier at the same address.

Oliver H. "Zeno" Hilton died December 15, 1977 and is buried in Woodlawn Cemetery.

Sources:

"Zeno, the River Kid" by Frank Tripp, The Kingston (NY) *Daily Freeman*, 16 January 1956, page 9.
1920, 1930, 1940 New York census

Email from Lu Randall.

About the authors and this book....

James Hare is a retired teacher of American History and Government from the Elmira City School District. He is also a former mayor and councilman for the City of Elmira.

He co-authored the book *Images of America, Elmira* with former county historian J. Arthur Kieffer.

Diane Janowski is the current Elmira City historian. She is also the editor of *New York History Review*, and was formerly the editor of the *Chemung Historical Journal*.

She has written many books about Elmira and Chemung County history, and co-authored the book *Images of America, The Chemung Valley* with Allen C. Smith.

Hare and Janowski are freelance writers for the Elmira *Star-Gazette*. Since 2014, they each write monthly articles on the history of the city of Elmira, New York. This book is a selection of their articles.

Be sure to look for our next book!

TRUE STORIES

of Elmira, New York

Volume 2

By Diane Janowski & James Hare